A Different Kind of Perfect

A Different Kind of Perfect

WRITINGS BY PARENTS ON RAISING A CHILD WITH SPECIAL NEEDS

Edited by Bernadette Thomas
and Cindy Dowling

Chapter introductions by Neil Nicoll

 Trumpeter · Boston · 2006

Trumpeter Books
An imprint of Shambhala Publications, Inc.
Horticultural Hall
300 Massachusetts Avenue
Boston, Massachusetts 02115
www.shambhala.com

Originally published under the title *Lessons from My Child: Parents' Experiences of Life with a Disabled Child*.

Published by arrangement with Finch Publishing, Australia.

9 8 7 6 5 4 3 2 1

First Trumpeter Edition

Printed in the United States of America

⊚ This edition is printed on acid-free paper that meets the American National Standards Institute z39.48 Standard. Distributed in the United States by Random House, Inc., and in Canada by Random House of Canada Ltd

Designed by Graciela Galup

Library of Congress Cataloging-in-Publication Data

Lessons from my child.
    A different kind of perfect: writings by parents on raising a child with special needs / edited by Bernadette Thomas and Cindy Dowling; chapter introductions by Neil Nicoll.—1st Trumpeter ed.
        p.   cm.
    Originally published: Lessons from my child. Lane Cove, NSW: Finch, c2004.
    Includes bibliographical references and index.
    ISBN-13: 978-1-59030-307-8 (pbk.: alk. paper)
    ISBN-10: 1-59030-307-5
    1. Children with disabilities—Family relationships.   2. Children with disabilities—Care.   3. Parents of children with disabilities.   4. Parent and child.   5. Parenting.   I. Thomas, Bernadette, 1960–   II. Dowling, Cindy.   III. Title.

HQ773.6.L47   2006
306.874087—dc22

                                                    2006014922

For the parents who gave us their stories,
and for Richard and Nicholas,
who gave us the inspiration

Let Us Have Faith

Security is mostly a superstition.
It does not exist in nature, nor do the children
    of men as a whole experience it.
Avoiding danger is no safer in the long run
    than outright exposure.
Life is either a daring adventure, or nothing.
To keep our faces toward change and behave
    like free spirits
In the presence of fate is strength undefeatable.

HELEN KELLER

Contents

Laughter

PREFACE

Cindy Dowling

AT SOME POINT in everyone's life there exists a defining moment, a splinter of absolute clarity that takes us back from the edge and, at least momentarily, parts the fog of discontent and confusion that so often obscures our view of life.

The genesis of this moment is different for us all. For some, it comes from something as simple as a touch, a forgotten perfume, the chorus of a favorite song, a view from an unfamiliar window.

My moment of clarity came when I began researching material for this book. As anyone who has ever typed the phrase "disabled children" into a Google search knows, there is an overwhelming volume of disability-related information on the Internet. Somehow, amid the chat rooms and miracle cures, I found a poem by Helen Keller entitled "Let Us Have Faith."

As I read, I realized that Ms. Keller had managed to distill my myriad emotions about raising a disabled child into six carefully crafted lines. I was reminded once again of the comfort that can be found in the words of others who have shared similar experiences and of why I and my coauthors were so determined to see this project succeed.

The poem begins:

> Security is mostly a superstition.
> It does not exist in nature, nor do the children of men
>   as a whole experience it.

A recent report estimates that 7.5 million members of the U.S. population can be classified as "retarded." In Australia, the Autism

Association believes that one in every 100 children will be born with an autism spectrum disorder. A thousand individuals are born with cystic fibrosis in the United States every year, while ten children in every ten thousand live births will have Down syndrome. In the United Kingdom, 8.7 million citizens suffer from some degree of hearing impairment, more than one million are registrable as blind or partially sighted, and 1,800 babies are diagnosed with cerebral palsy every year. In total, 360,000 children are born with a recognized disability in the United Kingdom annually. Across the developed world, three in every one thousand children will suffer cerebral palsy; three in a thousand will be born with a significant hearing impairment.

In spite of the statistics, people with disabilities remain one of the most misunderstood and marginalized sectors on earth. The world as a whole remains uneasy with the "less than perfect."

Before a baby's arrival, every parent has certain expectations for his or her offspring. Ballet lessons or Boy Scouts, blue eyes or red hair; perhaps a sense of humor like dad or a sweet singing voice like mom. Astronaut, farmer, actress, chef, rock star, or rodeo rider—all things are possible. We take for granted that our children will do what everyone's children do—go to school, leave home, get a job, marry, and in turn have children of their own.

But those certainties come to an abrupt end for some parents soon after their child is born. Instead of the perfect, "healthy" baby expected, they find themselves with a special-needs child.

It is then that these parents begin to pay the high price of society's discomfort with the disabled. Despite a desperate need for support, family, friends, and professionals alike often meet the plight of parents with bewilderment, ignorance, or—worst of all—pity. Rather than being offered information and guidance about their child's disability, parents are usually forced to seek it out themselves, playing medical detective at a time when their emotional lives are in tremendous upheaval.

In compiling the stories for this book, the most common response we had from parents with a newborn special-needs child was how lonely they felt, how singular and cut off from the rest of the world they believed themselves to be.

Along with a sense of isolation, parents often find themselves battling one of the great myths of disability, which I refer to as the Madonna and Child complex. In an effort to deflect an often harsh reality, society prefers to sugarcoat the truth about raising a special-needs child, to the lasting detriment of both parents and the children themselves.

Film and television are the most obvious indicators of how children with disabilities have been cast into the role of naive, incorruptible innocents rather than the living, breathing, real human beings they are. Films such as *Rain Man* succeed in making autism seem like a rather endearing personality disorder; Leonardo Di Caprio played the intellectually disabled son in *What's Eating Gilbert Grape?* mostly for laughs; while appearances of the slow-witted, "gentle giant" Down syndrome child on the screen are too numerous to mention. The physically disabled, the blind, the deaf, and the seriously ill—all are cast in the role of virtuous victim, politely waiting to be saved by more able-bodied rescuers.

Parents suffer a similar fate. How often are they—particularly mothers—painted as selfless martyrs, quasi-tragic figures who accept their fate stoically and with a minimum of fuss?

The truth is, of course, that neither image is correct. Disabled children are no more pure of spirit than any other child—they are as prone to anger, selfishness, greed, and spite as their non-disabled peers. Similarly, I have yet to meet a parent of a special-needs child who qualifies for sainthood. The parents I have met, and the ones whom you will meet within these pages, are ordinary people, women and men who have found themselves with a child and a life not necessarily of their choosing, but who continue to do the best they can with what they have. It is survival and the desire to be happy that drive them, not bravery or some strange need for martyrdom.

Sentimentalizing the truth of raising a child with disabilities demeans both parents and offspring, and often creates more stress for those parents still coming to terms with their child's diagnosis. It is not uncommon for parents, reared on the Hollywood version of disability, to feel as though they aren't reacting to their predicament in the "right" way. If there is one message that comes through loud and clear from our parent contributors, it is that there is no right way to react to the birth and upbringing of a special-needs child, no template for coping. There is only your way.

> Avoiding danger is no safer in the long run than
>   outright exposure.
> Life is either a daring adventure, or nothing.

The process of compiling this book really began several years ago when publisher and first-time mom Bernadette Thomas was informed that her newborn son, Richard, had Down syndrome. Once the initial stages of shock and denial had eased, Bernadette did what countless parents have done before her in the past—she began searching for as much information as she could about her child's condition and what she might be able to expect in the years to come.

While the medical information proved to be voluminous, Bernadette was soon struck by the lack of material on the one subject she desperately needed to know more about—what could she expect from life with a disabled child? Was the roller coaster ride of emotions she suffered through normal? Was there anyone else who could relate to her feelings? Where were the voices of the parents like herself, those who had been forced to leave their expectations behind in the hospital delivery room and forge a new reality for themselves and their families?

Bernadette did find a handful of parent support books, but drew little comfort from them. By and large they were overtly sentimental, full of lofty ideals and syrupy catchphrases. The overall message of the books was clear and unsatisfactory: parents should be strong and count their blessings for the gift of these special little angels into their lives. Little mention was ever made

of sleepless nights, endless tears, fear, frustration, or a life domi-
nated by medical appointments and hospital dates, the way life
really is for millions of parents.

Realizing the need to allow people like herself to be heard,
Bernadette set about collecting real stores from real people. Along
with the stories, she also picked up a little help. I offered to join
the project while I was considering writing a story about my son,
Nicholas, who is autistic. A slightly later arrival was Neil Nicoll,
a psychologist with the Vern Barnett School for Children with
Autism. Neil has spent many years counseling parents who have
just received the news every parent dreads—that their child has a
disability. His tremendous clinical knowledge, coupled with his
great empathy for parents and their families, made him a natural
choice when we realized the need to include some professional
advice among the parent stories. Neil's dedication to this project
has been unswerving and his contribution invaluable.

The parent stories in this book are grouped under the categories of grief, denial, anger, depression, acceptance, empowerment, marriage, family and friends, love and joy, spirituality, and
laughter. The decision to divide the book this way came from the
need to provide readers with a structured format. The placement
of individual stories within certain subject headings is admittedly
rather arbitrary. Some contributions listed under "Grief" could
well be interchangeable with others contained in the "Acceptance" chapter, for instance. We realize that no emotion exists in
isolation. Our hope is that by highlighting the various emotional
responses of parents, the degree to which having a special-needs
child is a continually life-altering experience will be clear to
readers.

To keep our faces toward change and behave like free
spirits in the presence of fate is strength undefeatable.

When Bernadette and I began advertising for stories, we braced
ourselves for a flood of contributions. There were so many parents
affected by their child's disability, we knew, and so little written

from their viewpoint. Surely thousands would be rushing to put pen to paper? In fact the flood was more like a trickle. A story here, a story there, lots of tentative inquiries that resulted in nothing. Men, in particular, proved to be elusive contributors. While some were happy to share a resume of their child's diagnosis and prognosis, the task of describing how their child's disability impacted them at an emotional level proved overwhelming for most. In the end, it took more than two years for all the stories contained here to be collected.

It wasn't until Bernadette and I sat down to write our own stories for inclusion that we realized why others had not been more forthcoming. Writing about your child's disability is damned hard. It takes you to places you don't necessarily want to go. It opens old wounds and summons new fears. It forces you to confront yourself, to gaze into the mirror and write down what you see. For most of us, the face that stares back is not always the one we show to the world.

Every parent who has contributed to this book has found the courage to expose that face. Placing their trust in two complete strangers, these people have given us an unforgettable insight into their lives. The stories are as different as the people who have written them. Our contributors come from around the world, including the United States, Europe, Australia, Canada, and Singapore. Some are wealthy, others are not. Some are highly educated, others left school as soon as they could. Some are in happy partnerships, others prefer to go it alone.

Every emotion, from overwhelming despair to wry humor, is contained within these stories. Some parents seem to have reached a level of acceptance about their child. Others are still clearly battling to make sense of it all. Every one of them tells it like it is, warts and all.

Ultimately, each story stands as a reaffirmation of the strongest bond of all—that of a parent's love for their child. Every one of them has left an indelible impression on Bernadette, Neil, and me and will, we trust, on every reader.

There are many people who should read this book. For professionals involved in counseling, respite care, or disability support services, Neil offers some invaluable guidelines for dealing with client issues. For medical professionals, the parent stories will help put a human face on a patient diagnosis.

For those who have a relative or friend raising a disabled child, the book will provide you with some rudimentary tools for understanding and insight into an often hidden emotional world.

If you are the parent of a special-needs child, then you should know that this book was written specifically with you in mind. It was our aim, and the aim of every parent who sat down to write, that you know you are not alone. We want you to know that your emotions are valid, that your battles are not hopeless, that your triumphs are celebrated, and that you are understood, perhaps not by the greater society, but by millions of other mothers, fathers, and caretakers from every corner of the world.

It is our hope that you take comfort in the contents of this book, and if you should find within it a moment of clarity, so much the better.

Grief

Sorrows cannot all be explained away . . .
in a life truly lived, grief and loss accumulate
like possessions.

STEPHAN KANFER

Introduction

NEIL NICOLL

GRIEF COMES TO EVERY single one of us at some stage of our lives. It is one of the few emotional states that all societies acknowledge through ritual and ceremony—a Christian funeral or Hindu cremation are first and foremost socially instituted ways of allowing people to express their sorrow.

But how does grief manifest when nobody has died? This is the dilemma that faces the parents of children with disabilities.

Definition

Grief is most clearly defined as a personal and emotional reaction to a significant loss, most commonly the death of a loved one or involvement in some unforeseen tragedy. But it is not always physical loss that brings about grieving. Grief can also flow from the loss of dreams and ideas, hopes and expectations—the loss of what might have been. It is in this sense that grief is commonly associated with the birth of a child with a disability or the later discovery that a child has a disabling condition.

Critical to any examination of the grief process is the realization that it is an intensely individual experience. No two people will experience and express grief in exactly the same way, and there is no "right" way to behave while in a state of mourning.

The Stages of Grief

Despite its personal nature, there are a number of general stages that most people pass through on the road to accepting a significant loss. These stages can briefly be described as follows:

Shock—A stage often characterized by feelings of numbness or disbelief. People often report feeling "paralyzed," distant, or even disconnected from the reality of their situation. In extreme cases, those in shock may even experience sensory distortions.

Denial/anger—As unhealthy as these emotions may appear at face value, both in fact mark the beginning of emotional healing. Both anger and denial will be examined in greater detail in later chapters.

Pining and reminiscence—When people grieve as the result of a loved one's death, this stage is defined by increased feelings of preoccupation with the deceased. Frequent visits to the cemetery, spending hours gazing at old photographs, letters, or personal belongings, feeling the "presence" of the deceased or even asking their advice when problems occur—all these are examples of reminiscence. Dwelling on old regrets and past guilt involving the deceased are a common feature of this stage. However, in the case of parents experiencing grief at the diagnosis of a disability, this stage is a little more difficult to define. The guilt feelings in this instance are more likely to arise from a sense of failure and regret at the loss of previous expectations. Some parents attempt to compensate for this guilt by working tirelessly on their child's educational and therapeutic needs and by making the disabled child the family's number-one priority at all times. Ironically, this strident dedication may in fact ultimately lead to even more feelings of guilt as the parent realizes the child is not improving or the needs of the rest of the family are being neglected.

Toward acceptance—At this stage, people begin to reorganize their lives, refocus their energies, and get on with life. New relationships may be formed, new hobbies begun. Again, for those with disabled children, reaching a point of acceptance is not so clear-cut. Because of the immense demands often placed on parents after diagnosis, many find themselves too busy to grieve. With the grieving process delayed in this way, acceptance for many parents becomes harder to attain and maintain. A later chapter is devoted to discussing acceptance more fully.

The Chronic-Sorrow Theory

One widely accepted theory on the grief process of parents with disabled children is the notion of chronic sorrow. First suggested by Olshansky in 1962, the theory suggests that the typical stages of grief outlined above do not necessarily apply to those who mourn something other than the death of a loved one. Instead, parents may not necessarily ever achieve real acceptance but instead remain in a state of emotional flux, at times appearing content with their lives, at other times (such as the child's birthday or following a bad school report), returning to full-fledged grief for a time.

If that all sounds a little grim, it needn't be. Most theorists agree that chronic sorrow is a normal psychological reaction and should not be viewed as a lapse back into denial or shock. Put simply, people return to their grief from time to time simply because the source of their grief—in this instance, a disabled child—remains a tangible presence in their life.

Coping with Grief

Grief-stricken people have no greater enemy than themselves. When we grieve, the emotional pain often leaves us with little energy to take care of our physical needs, and may blind us to those who are trying to help.

Grief-stricken people have no greater enemy than themselves.

A period of emotional pain often drives people toward increased use of alcohol, cigarettes, tranquilizers, and antidepressants as a means of helping them cope. Although the temptation to forget your troubles for a while can be strong, a clear head and good health will serve you much better in the long term.

As difficult as it can be, it is important that you eat right and get regular exercise.

Remember that while we may grieve alone, we heal with one another. Grief is an isolating emotion, so it is important that you remember those who are there to share your burden. Talk about your feelings and don't be afraid to ask for help if you need it.

Avoid making important decisions at this time. People overwhelmed with sorrow are generally not thinking with a normal degree of rationality. Grief can sometimes cause impulsive or "out of character" behavior, so put off making any big changes in your life until your pain has subsided.

Realize that although time doesn't necessarily heal all wounds, it certainly lessens their pain. Accept that you may experience periods of grief for years to come, but also realize that you will equally experience periods of great happiness, humor, and contentment.

Everything and Nothing at All

Cindy Dowling

She was whip thin and had pale blue eyes that glittered like little moist diamonds, but it is her voice I will always recall most clearly. Cruel and loud, that voice seemed to resonate through the electrical-appliance showroom, an accusatory bell, ringing out my shame and failure for all to hear.

"What on earth is wrong with that child?" she demanded to know. "He almost opened a fridge door right in my face!" She smelled of recent cigarettes and old perfume. Her vowels were as flat as roadkill.

Together we turned to stare at the source of her outrage. A little yellow-haired boy, cheeks colored with effort and chocolate, was rushing madly along an aisle of refrigerators, flinging open doors with obvious delight.

"Nicholas!" I said sharply, although I knew that any words I had for him were wasted. My pretense at control was really for the benefit of the glaring woman at my side, and perhaps for some shadowy part of my own mind that still dared to hope for such things.

I hurried over to my son and grabbed his arms. "No, leave the doors alone," I told him, still all too aware of my audience. It was, of course, my fault. At five, Nicholas was as hyperactive and non-compliant as a child going through the Terrible Twos. He raced across roads without looking, hurled himself off any object he could find to climb, and found it impossible to sit still for more than a few minutes at a time. I knew he needed constant supervision. It was just that I was so damned tired all the time.

Nicholas began to squeal and slap my hands in an attempt to

be released. I looked up and saw the woman still staring at us and wondered vaguely how many other people were furtively watching our little show.

"I'm very sorry. He doesn't mean to do it. He's autistic." There. I'd said it. Told the truth and thrown myself on the mercy of the court. It usually worked. But this time the judge was having none of it.

"And what exactly does that mean?" she sneered.

What exactly does autism mean? Right then, overwhelmed by embarrassment and the sounds of my child's despair, I didn't have an answer for that woman. Now, six years later, a little wiser, and a lot tougher, I know precisely what I should have told her.

In fact I have written her a letter, this woman whose name I never knew and who I will most likely never meet again. She will, of course, never read it. It doesn't matter. She dared to judge my child and me and found us both guilty. We, the condemned, demand the right of reply.

To the woman in the shop, September 1996:

You asked me a question once that I couldn't answer. Now I can. What does it mean to have an autistic child?

It means watching the beautiful, perfect baby you gave birth to, who carried all the usual hopes and dreams and proud ambitions that parents bestow on their children, quietly slip away, a little piece at a time, until all those dreams have utterly disappeared.

It means having to learn to live with and accept a stranger who wears your child's face—a ghost who prefers staring at blank walls to picture books, who never meets your gaze or seeks your touch, who is driven by urges and instincts that nobody else can begin to comprehend.

Autism means the bleak realization that a mother's love isn't always enough.

Autism means quiet tears at three A.M. It means unexpected joy at the smallest of life's mercies: a crooked smile, a shirt buttoned, a word remembered, a name scrawled uncertainly on a piece of paper.

It means often feeling isolated and being misunderstood, even by those who love you best. It means experiencing the very best and the very worst that other people can be. It means discovering coldness in the hearts of friends and immense kindness in the smiles of relative strangers. It means discovering that there are many worse things than being different, but none worse than being ignorant.

Autism means receiving praise when all you really want is help, pity when all you really need is rest.

Having an autistic child means realizing that even the most learned of doctors can be a fool and the most qualified of teachers can be ignorant.

It means still believing in miracles even though you know the time for miracles is long past. Autism means secret prayers to a god you are no longer sure of.

Autism means frustration, humiliation, sorrow, confusion, helplessness, and beneath them all, a slow-burning sense of rage at the injustice of it all. To have an autistic child is to fear the future, not because it is uncertain but because it is so lacking in possibilities.

Autism means years of bitter denial before finally finding the peace that comes with acceptance. It means learning that perfection is a myth and homogeneity is to be fought against. It means understanding that humanity's real triumph is diversity, not uniformity.

Autism means telling your child you love him and realizing that, despite the years of pain and despair, you truly mean every word you say.

What does autism mean? The answer is simple. It means everything and nothing at all.

Witnessing

Anna Stewart

I SIT CROSS-LEGGED ON THE FLOOR of the playroom. Eighteen-month-old Sabrina moves closer and looks at me. She picks up a green crayon. I do the same. She says "uh," and holds the crayon over her head. I do the same. I wait until she brings her hand down before I bring down mine. She is the leader, this is her dance, and I am here to follow her every step. She picks up another crayon, a blue one, and taps both crayons on the floor. The carpet muffles their sound, so she awkwardly gets up and totters to the low table and tries again. I take another crayon—mine is purple—and crawl over to the table. *Bang, bang,* go her crayons. "Eee," she says. And "Eee," I go. She becomes aware of the game now and realizes that she is in charge.

She looks at me to see what I will do. She bangs the crayons on the table again, then raises them over her head, then bangs them back on the table. I follow every gesture, mimic every sound. Her smile stretches past her face and into my heart. She is making more sounds now, "naa" and "uh-ee." She laughs when she discovers that there are no limits. She stands up and plops down on the carpet, then laughs from the root of her being. Tears come to my own eyes as I realize what I am doing. I am her witness. I am here to listen to her in her world in her way. I am the first person in her life to witness her this thoroughly.

Sabrina has developmental delays. She is only just starting to walk. She has no words and she can't use a spoon yet. Yet, in this moment, she is being seen for who she is, not who she will be or who she should be. Just her, my sweet baby girl. I cry as I realize what a gift this is, for me to be her witness. All of us, every one of us, needs this, to be both witnessed and to give witness. Words aren't necessary. Only the act of being here for another. No judgment, no concerns, no opinions at all.

Everything changed in that moment for me. I still get frustrated with my daughter. I still get resentful of her neediness. But from that moment on I understood her. I understood she was doing the best she could. In that moment, it was enough.

A year later and it wasn't enough. Sabrina still did not have words. She pointed at things she wanted. She used grunts and sounds. She used eye contact and touching to get people's attention. She communicated in many ways, but not with words. I told people she was much younger than she was.

It kills me, her lack of language. Everything else I can handle. I define myself with my language, but she does not. I live by my words, work with them, connect and love through them. I know my sons by what they talk to me about. I can comfort their bad dreams. Offer to listen when they need to work out a social problem. We can talk about our plans, our dreams, and our memories. Sabrina cannot share that with us, and it hurts me.

Sometimes grief infuses me when I am reminded that she is not normal, and I wring my heart out with worry that she may never be a typical kid. She looks like the other kids, but she runs with a lopsided gait. She is healthy and yet she doesn't appear to understand at least half of what is said to her. It's almost as if her body is communicating but not yet her mind. She alternates between being cheerful, excited, and willing and being whiny, clingy, and frustrated. I notice that I do too. Some days I feel blessed and some days I feel paralyzed with heartache. It's hard to always pay attention to what she needs and wants and to pay attention to my own needs and wants as well. Her, me, my two sons, husband, parents, family, friends, schools . . . we all live with special needs.

Some days I feel blessed and some days I feel paralyzed with heartache.

I was not shocked when the therapy team at the hospital told me she had delays. Obviously I knew she wasn't developing normally—that's why I'd come in. They could not offer a reason, or a cause, or an idea of what the future would hold for her. I was never shocked, but still I have grieved; I have been spurred by guilt into action, demanding more services. And I have wept for all that isn't and all that is.

As she gets older and more able—dressing herself in her own pink outfits, trying to draw faces, getting her own yogurt and spoon—I have learned to stop telling people she is younger than she is. Sabrina doesn't mind, she never did. It was my problem, not hers. She is happy, she lives in the moment. All is well in Sabrina's world. I carry the burden for both of us. I worry and weep, despair and deny, laugh and love. It is my job, my agreement with her. I offer her a witness and she gives me back my own deep breaths. I have stopped lying about her.

I stood as she was born. She slipped from my body like a sea otter, breathing in the salty air of the ocean's womb. She cried for over an hour, longer than the whole birth. She was nearly ten pounds, with full lips and long legs. My friend Danae, who witnessed us, told me she had never seen a woman stand in her own truth like I did to birth my girl. I felt like a Hindu goddess, holding a sword, a spoon, a pen, and a magic wand in my four powerful arms. I knew, even then, that this was no ordinary daughter. And that I would need those four arms to mother her.

I tell the truth now about everything. I tell it because I am no longer capable of lying. It's been slashed out of me through this journey in the special-needs world. But the main reason I tell the truth is that Sabrina understands the difference. I can't lie about her age—she knows she is four and that she had a tea party with her girlfriends for her birthday. Sabrina started to talk. She told me that the pea soup I gave her was "yucky." She tells me she wants waffles instead of oatmeal for breakfast. She tells me that she went out and played in the snow with her brothers and it was fun.

Her words are still blurry, like she's coming up for air. But I can understand her most of the time. I have learned to listen without words. But the only way I can do it is to stay true to who I am. That is the only way I can fully witness her. I can only really see her if my own eyes are clear, my own hands clean, and my own heart present. And perhaps, some day, she will tell me her dreams. But for now, as she leaves for school, she cheerfully calls out, "Gye, ee ou ater." And I am grateful to be her mother. Most days, it is enough.

Shattered Dreams

Annie Hedberg

Had I known the pain and tragedy that awaited me on September 30, 1999, I would never have left home that morning.

I was a divorced twenty-four-year-old mother with two beautiful daughters. Cassidy was three and a half, and Kailee was eighteen months old. At 3:37 P.M. that afternoon I got the phone call that flipped my world completely upside down.

The voice on the other end of the line told me that Kailee had been in an accident and was being flown to a children's hospital. She had nearly hung herself on a rope swing while playing with Cassidy and her cousins at my sister's house. She had been without oxygen for more than ten minutes.

After a few hours of confusion I was allowed to see my daughter. I walked through the closed doors of the pediatric intensive care unit and into utter tragedy. I'd driven past this section of the hospital so many times in my life and never stopped to think about the pain that occurred within its walls. Everywhere there were tiny children hooked up to tubes and machines. Doctors, nurses, and parents hurried to and fro.

In the midst of it all was my baby. The doctors had fought for hours to save her life. Kailee had tubes of every kind in and on her. I later learned what they were all for. Some of the tubing was for life support, but I didn't know this until a few days later.

I was in a complete state of shock. I remember thinking that she looked fine, not badly hurt at all, and convincing myself that this whole episode would soon be over and my baby would be home with me in a few days, just like before. Kailee cried and reached out for me, her neck bruised and her little feet still smudged with playground dirt.

I soon learned how deceptive appearances could be. The doctors told me that although she looked normal right then, her brain had not yet begun to swell. This was a process that took seventy-two hours, and until the swelling had taken place and gone down, it was impossible for them to predict whether or not Kailee would ever be her normal self again. She could, I was told, emerge from the swelling either completely recovered or severely brain damaged. She could even die. There was no way for them to tell, and there was nothing they could do to prevent any brain damage from occurring.

For a mother to hear something like that is indescribable. I felt such rage and such sadness, and incredible disbelief that all I could do was sit and watch while my daughter suffered alone. Mothers are supposed to be able to fix things for their children. But there was nothing I could do for Kailee.

A few days later the news came that I'd been dreading. Most of Kailee's brain had been severely and irreparably damaged. Alone in a room full of doctors, I listened as they told me my daughter would either die without life support, or if she did survive away from the machines, she would be in a permanently vegetative state.

I was calm in my response. Asking them to take good care of her while I was away, I left the hospital for the first time since the accident. I went home and let my heart break. I had just been told that the baby who made me laugh, who loved her sister so much, and who gave us such joy had died. The Kailee who remained would never be the same, yet I wouldn't be allowed to mourn that loss because her little body was still left behind and needed my care and attention.

I don't know that I could have felt any more hurt and survived the pain. I knew even then that people would not understand how profound was my loss. My baby was gone. That night I collapsed, I threw up, I raged and cried. I don't know how I made it through. Later I called my parents and asked them to come to my house so I could tell them. They didn't believe me, in fact no one fully accepted the extent of what I was telling them. They all thought I was overreacting, exaggerating. That made my world an even lonelier place. With no one to turn to, I cried alone all night long.

I realized that awful night that it wasn't a matter of not being able or willing to take care of Kailee that was distressing me so deeply. I still loved my child. But all the dreams and hopes that I had allowed myself to dream for her were now gone. Kailee would not be going to school with her big sister, she would not learn to drive, she would not get married or go to college.

... all the dreams and hopes that I had allowed myself to dream for her were now gone.

By next morning I knew that while I couldn't control what had happened, I could control my attitude and approach to the tragedy. I decided then and there to learn everything I could about my new little Kailee. I spent hours in medical libraries, I cross-examined doctors, I had three months at the hospital with my daughter learning all I could about her condition and treatment.

My attitude to my new Kailee is that I am realistically optimistic. I've learned to relax a little too. When it was time to pick out wheelchairs, the therapists were very apprehensive about asking me to do this. When I asked them why, they told me that a lot of parents have a hard time with this. I laughed and said, "The way I look at it, I will get all of the best parking spots!"

After Kailee's accident everything in my life changed. I sold my home and moved in with my parents. I quit my job to take care of Kailee. The man I was dating at the time told me he could not handle having a handicapped child for the rest of his life.

The first few months home from the hospital were the hardest. I felt alone. Nobody really understood what I was going through. Even Kailee's father didn't want anything to do with us. Kailee had to be taken to therapy twice a day, five days a week. She didn't sleep but moaned and cried twenty hours a day. She took so much medication, I had to write up a schedule to keep track of it. I remember one night lying on my bedroom floor just screaming to my Heavenly Father, asking him to help make Kailee sleep. "I can't do this for one more day," I told him.

But of course I did survive. It's been more than two years since Kailee's accident and I'm in a much better place. I've gotten remarried to a very supportive man, and we have a new baby.

As for Kailee, she hasn't really changed since that first day in the hospital. Actually she has gotten a little worse. Kailee cannot talk, walk, see, swallow, move, or communicate. But somehow we have learned her language. I still have my moments when I watch my two other daughters playing together and I have to hide my face so that nobody will see my tears. I think of how Kailee would have loved to join in these games with her sisters. Sometimes the pain still hits me like a punch in the guts.

Despite it all, I am grateful for this experience. I have learned so much about myself and met the most wonderful friends along the way. I have learned a whole new language and way of living.

Editors' note: While this book was in production, Kailee died. Anne has added a short postscript:

> I often think, since Kailee passed away, what it would be like if she were healthy or if this had never happened. But I realize that I would not give up what I have been given. I am so grateful for all that Kailee's disability has given me. I thought she would live a lot longer than she did. I think maybe she went when she did because I got to a place where I would have loved to take care of her for the rest of my life. I loved it, even though the day-to-day was hard as hell! It is the things you hate the most that you will miss the most when they are gone. The things I miss about Kailee are her yelling moans, her feed bag beeping, her twisted little body . . .
>
> I miss you, angel baby, so much. Run, jump, sing, and yell now simply because you can—and know that your mama loves you.

Disappointment

Jennifer Beitz

Disappointment. That was my overriding emotion the moment I saw my newborn daughter for the very first time. I felt like I had received a gift that I didn't ask for. My husband and I both sat in the hospital room in tears as the geneticist confirmed she had Down syndrome.

I have never cried so much in my entire life as I did that first month. My grief was overwhelming as I realized my daughter would never be the child I had been expecting. She would never have children of her own. As a mother of five, I suffered greatly from that knowledge, and my copious tears were for my daughter's loss as much as my own.

Being a nurse, I knew I had to grieve the loss of a "perfect" child. And grieve I did. Every time I was alone, I cried. I did most of my grieving in the car on the way to and from the hospital. There was little privacy in her hospital room, and I had other children at home who needed a strong mother, not a grief-stricken wreck. I quickly realized that despite my anguish, life went on. Homework had to be gone over, meals prepared, children tucked into bed at night. I held my tears in check whenever I could and unleashed them in a torrent of despair when nobody was watching.

The relationship between mother and child is both mysterious and profound. Although I had been so anguished by my daughter's disability, by the time we left the hospital after her first surgery, I already felt an incredible bond with her. My daughter hadn't yet smiled or even responded to me in any way, but I soon felt great love for her and a desire to deal with the challenges life had handed us both.

I felt excited that I could handle the challenge of a child with special needs. My husband felt much the same way that I did. There is a special bond between a parent and a child and it becomes even stronger when your child has special needs.

Now that my daughter is healthy, I feel extremely blessed to have a child with Down syndrome. I don't think I could have said that before I had her. I used to feel sorry for people with children with special needs. Now I am one of those people and I certainly don't feel sorry for myself, or need anyone else's pity.

I feel like God gave us an extra-special child to love and care for. She is the darling of the family. Some days I feel sad about things she may not be able to do. I see a child her age doing so much more than she is capable of. I find myself crying more easily now.

I see my daughter as the gift I never thought to ask for. She is the greatest gift of all. We are all learning more from her than we can ever teach her.

A Blessing or a Nightmare?

Sindoor Desai

Sujeet, twenty-one years old, four feet eleven inches tall, and handsome in his black tux, red bow tie and red cummerbund, ends his hour-long performance with his signature piece, "Memory" from *Cats,* and takes a bow. After a few seconds of pin-drop silence the entire audience stands with overwhelming cheering and applause. Suj, with his eyes shining and a wide smile, takes another bow. Then he stands tall, waves at the still-standing audience, and leaves the stage.

Before he leaves, his eyes search for his mom and dad in the audience. When he sees them clapping, smiling, and nodding with approval, he gives them a thumbs-up and says, "*Yes*!! I did it, Mom." His mom, with pounding heart, tearful eyes, choked voice, but great pride, wants to savor that moment and wishes it would last forever.

Twenty-one years ago, when the team of doctors and nurses walked into the hospital room, a sudden chill of cold ran through my veins, and my ears started to freeze as I heard the diagnosis of my newborn baby. The baby who had such a beautiful pink glow but was helplessly hanging in their hands like a rag doll! Yes, just like it is described in the medical books when they write about Down syndrome. My second son, to whom I had just given birth, was labeled in that room "a disabled child born with Down syndrome"! They announced his entire medical condition in two sentences: "There is not much we can do with these children. Just take him home and do the best you can." Period!

At that point everyone went away, leaving me and my husband alone in the room. They took our newborn son for further blood work and tests. My husband and I, despite our medical backgrounds, just sat there stunned. The first thing that flashed through our minds was the list of conditions we had studied in our pathology books under the rubric "Mental Retardation" and how, among the top ten in that list, was Down syndrome. There was no information in these medical books or from the hospital staff regarding these children's social life nor what to do for them nor what to expect when we brought them home to nurture.

We suddenly realized that not only was our newborn son pigeonholed, but we, along with our other son, Ninad, were instantly labeled a "special family." Always worried, tired, ashamed, feeling guilty, you name it, no matter what special characteristics special parents manifested, we displayed every one of them. Instantly our life changed, and it did so forever.

My husband and I seemed to forget how to laugh, and we weren't able to appreciate even the simple joys of daily life. Until the day Suj was born, everyone thought I was such a soft-spoken person—they said they could not even tell that I was around. However, after Sujeet's birth I started yelling all the time, so loudly and so often that I brought tears to Ninad's eyes. The guilt continues to this day for not doing justice to Ninad, who unfortunately became the victim and was labeled a "special sibling" to his "special" brother.

Before Suj was born, we'd had a large circle of friends to whom we showed off Ninad and whose praise we immensely enjoyed hearing. Proud parents, we were floating on clouds of joy and contentment, when suddenly, with the birth of Suj two years later, the cloud burst and brought us down to earth. It was as if someone had slapped us right in the face, saying, "Aha . . . now tell us how proud you are!" Sujeet's birth ended that. We felt as if we were being punished for raving too much about Ninad. Unfortunately none of our friends or family was able to comfort us because getting together with them was no longer enjoyable for us.

Every time we took Sujeet along, the "look" he got from others felt hurtful and brought tears. We decided to avoid social gatherings where we had to bring our children. We started separating ourselves from our friends and family until we were totally isolated. We kept ourselves overburdened with work. My husband began working late hours, while I stayed up late reading whatever I could about Down syndrome. I spent endless hours researching the Internet, attending conferences and lectures, and I even published a couple of papers on dentistry and Down syndrome. I met with educators, trying to figure out why so much time is spent on writing individualized educational plans for these special children. Sitting at conference tables with school staff mostly listening to what my child could not do rather than what he could only added to the pain of Sujeet's limitations. I struggled to focus on mainstream issues but finally gave up, frustrated and disappointed at getting more denials than approvals, more rejections than acceptance. I was totally exhausted. I neglected my profession, my husband, and Ninad, who all needed me equally. Overwhelmed and possessed by the thought that no one except me could help Sujeet, I was aging rapidly.

Watching our boys grow up at opposite ends of the same rope, we began to appreciate the beauty of diversity. We learned the value of real friendship and peace in life. It was an eye-opener. Our total outlook toward humanity changed. This change was better for our personal growth, but was it better for us socially? We doubt that. We still are that special family who is isolated, advocating constantly for both our boys. We worry more about Suj. As much as we take pride in his accomplishments, we know that he would not have been where he is now without our constant advocacy. We worry about his well-being without us.

> *We worry about his well-being without us.*

There are two keys to Sujeet's current success. First, his passion for music. Second, and most important, is his desire to interact with other people and to have them to accept him just the way he is. I can certainly continue to support the first desire, but the second one, the acceptance from the community, is something I have no control over. Thinking about this has raised questions like "What will happen to Suj once we're gone? Who will care for him the way we do?," and has turned into a nightmare that we live with every day.

I would like to tell the hospital staff who told me with blank faces, that day that they gave me my son, "Do the best you can," that yes, I did the very best I could and I will continue to do so till my last breath, but it would have been easier and much more helpful if they had handed him to me that first day with some words of support and comfort.

Every night when we get into bed, Suj is still up wanting to watch TV. He gets into our bed, wrestles with his father, and then tucks us both under the blanket, giving us a big hug and a kiss. Then he leaves our room promising to take care of everything before he goes to bed and saying not to worry about a thing. Those hugs and kisses have magical strength. We hear him calling his brother, Ninad, and reminding him to make sure he studies and to keep Mom and Dad informed about his progress. After he checks his routine e-mails and the next day's weather forecast, he turns the computer off. He tucks his dog into his dog bed, turns on the security alarm, puts his CD in, and turns his bedroom lights off. In minutes, with the soothing tunes of Mozart coming from his room, we hear his deep breathing. We know he is fast asleep with no regrets and that the glow of full contentment on his face. In our bed, we pray to God for Sujeet's health and happiness and we thank him for blessing us with this unique child in our life.

However, despite the incredible joy he brings us, the last thought that still haunts us before we close our eyes at night is "What will become of Suj once we're gone?" We have no idea how to get rid of that nightmare.

Group

Colleen Kunkel

From the time my son was one month old, twice a week for eighteen months, I would pack him up and bring him to a center-based early-intervention program. The year was 1980 and things in the world of special education were very different. Parents of children with developmental disabilities would bring their child to a program where they (the parents) were educated about feeding techniques, positioning, and developmental milestones. It was expected that the parent would incorporate this learning into the infant's life on a continuing basis.

At these biweekly meetings the parents were required to meet with a social worker in a group setting while the children were receiving physical or occupational therapy. It was during these times that I became acquainted with a remarkable group of women. Sometimes in life you are thrown together with a group of people that you would otherwise not have met—thank God for those meetings! We'd speak about the enormous grief we were all dealing with and our feelings of loneliness. Over the months that passed, some new parents would join this group and others would leave. However, a certain core group would endure.

Upon completion of the early-intervention program many participants went on to preschool programs. It was no longer a requirement to meet with parents and share different stories and/or experiences, but this core group of women was not about to stop meeting. By now two years had passed. We had managed to get through the early years with one another's help, and we shared a very special bond. We began meeting monthly, at a different person's house each month. The hostess would provide the liquid refreshments and each attendee would bring an appetizer or dessert. What a wonderful way to continue to develop our newfound friendships.

Over the years we grew from being distraught women having children with developmental disabilities into strong advocates for our children and others. We have gone through various stages of denial and grief, along with anger and resentment. We also realized that we never knew when those stages might suddenly reappear. What began as a grieving parents' support group became a safe haven to express feelings that you wouldn't share with your closest family and friends. Very often you have feelings that you are embarrassed to admit to anyone. At Group you could speak of these feelings or thoughts with no worry of reprisal. Group took on a life of its own. Having someone and some place where you could express your most intimate feelings was a godsend. Support is important. We surrounded ourselves with others in similar situations as a way of dealing with our hardships and a way of learning from one another's experiences. I saw how important support is and how it has benefited me. And I now know I will never feel that loneliness again.

There have been times over the years where just talking, crying, or venting was not the answer. If we realized that one of us was not coming to terms with a certain situation and/or feelings, we would talk about it and the possible solutions. Some of us have used medication and therapy. Others might have retreated to a place called denial. Denial is a safe place and can be cathartic, but, to stay there too long is not the answer. There were also those who chose to tough it out. However anyone decided to deal with it, it took its toll on them and inevitably on their family and relationships.

It all boils down to the death of a dream. The dream of that perfect child you were expecting. I may never fully recover from that "death," but I have learned that you can go on and live a fulfilling life. Through Group we became stronger than we could have imagined, we developed friendships the likes of which I had never dreamed possible.

It is now twenty-two years later and the initial core Group is still together, along with other longtime members. We continue to confront obstacles and learn new things. Most of us have been dealing with the transition from school age to adult programming, while others are confronted with different group-home placements. Ironically, a few of us are employed by organizations pertaining to individuals with disabilities. All of us have become powerful advocates in our communities. This extraordinary Group of women would never have met had it not been mandatory to sit with a social worker during the early years.

Many positive changes have taken place within the service-delivery system over the years, but adequate support for parents continues to be lacking. It is a vital ingredient that needs to be addressed. Parents need parents who have walked in their shoes.

We still get together once a month. We are Group. Our families know not to make any requests of mom when Group is scheduled. We have supported each other through divorce, separation, cancer, breakdowns, lawsuits, chronic illness, physical assaults by our children, residential placements, hospitalizations, and of course the day-to-day inconveniences of life. This crazy Group of women have now forever bonded themselves together by getting a tattoo they designed during a weekend retreat. It symbolizes their children with disabilities—a heart with a teardrop.

Denial

Denial ain't just a river in Egypt.

Mark Twain

Introduction

NEIL NICOLL

PLACE A PERSON'S HAND momentarily over a naked flame and without exception their first impulse will be to jerk it away from the heat source—pronto.

Protecting ourselves from danger is one of the most basic and deeply rooted of all human instincts. But our self-protective urges are not confined to obvious external threats, such as fire, heights, or snakes.

Faced with tragic life-altering events such as the death of a spouse, unexpected and extreme physical violence, major illness, or the birth of a disabled child, our minds can respond by engaging in protective retreat, a complex, multifaceted mechanism most commonly termed denial. As in the case of the hand in the flame, our minds seek to protect us by removing us from the source of pain as quickly as possible.

What Is Denial?

Denial takes many forms and has almost as many definitions. In classical Freudian terms, denial is simply a defense mechanism that we employ to obscure or revoke our basest impulses. Later theorists, such as Carl Rogers, substantially expanded this definition, suggesting that people deny thoughts, facts, or events that are at odds with their own self-concept. A student who believes herself poor at spelling may regard an "A" on a spelling test a mere fluke. A man diagnosed with terminal cancer may refuse to believe that someone as healthy as himself could ever become so ill. A mother who gives birth to a physically handicapped child may insist that it couldn't be possible since no one in her family has ever suffered such a handicap before.

In its simplest form, denial is an attempt to put distance between our experience and ourselves. Denial is like a pain reliever that we take in an attempt to ease our anxiety via a subtle twist of our attention. In a sense, those in denial are saying, "This is not what I want! This is not what I expected!"

The End of Expectations

When a special-needs child is born, denial is one of the first emotions experienced by many families. The expectations surrounding the birth of a child are intensely personal and firmly held. There are few parents who haven't spent the nine months of pregnancy discussing their child's likely hair color, where they might go to school, whether they'll inherit Grandma's artistic talents or Uncle Bob's sense of humor.

The realization that those expectations may not or cannot be met can lead to strong feelings of bitterness for a time. Denial is a means of coping with that bitterness, of trying to make sense of a range of conflicting feelings and responses to very real and very stressful situations.

Denial occurs after the initial feelings of shock and numbness have dissipated. For some parents, denial may be acute, with expressions and actions anchored in disbelief lasting for months, even years. Parents who continue to dispute a child's diagnosis even after a second opinion has confirmed it, who resist enrolling the child in special-needs programs despite specialist advice to the contrary, who ignore major developmental delays or abnormal behaviors, may very well be in extended denial.

In fact, within the context of disability, it is not unusual for people to experience denial over a longer period of time than, for instance, someone experiencing the death of a loved one. When someone dies, there is a reluctant but nevertheless clearer understanding that their physical loss is not going to be recovered. Death is not reversible, and even the most grief stricken will eventually accept that obvious fact. However, for the parents of a special-needs child, there is no physical loss to speed up the process. Indeed, having daily contact with a living child often encourages hopes that one day the disability may be redressed, and in doing so, prolongs the denial process.

The Role of Guilt

Denial is a weapon with many triggers. For some parents, denial arises from a fundamental feeling of guilt at having had a child with a disability in the first place. Mothers may wonder if they've done something wrong during their pregnancy, or whether that epidural had some role to play, or indeed, whether they stopped breast-feeding too early or introduced solids too soon. Fathers may also ponder their role in the child's disability, and those from some cultures may also have issues linked to their masculinity and genetic heritage.

Families in Denial

Denial is not necessarily a singular response. Group denial is a well-documented phenomenon, and is often seen within family units—the "things like this don't happen in our family" syndrome.

Two anecdotes passed on to me by friends illustrate the ways in which entire families can go into denial about a child's disability. In the first, a woman who had spent several years coming to terms with her son's Down syndrome diagnosis left the child with her mother for the day. When she returned, the mother insisted the boy had performed a range of academic feats, such as counting to twenty and reciting the alphabet, that the mother knew her son was simply not yet capable of. The mother then insisted this proved that the boy was "only a little bit Down's."

Another mother recalled the time her father insisted that her highly agitated son could quickly be calmed "with a good smack," despite the fact that the child had had a diagnosis of severe autism for more than five years. The same father was also prone to claiming the child's temper tantrums were the results of "being spoiled."

Apart from illustrating how steadfast denial can be in the face of logic, both cases highlight the problems that can arise for parents when key family members maintain a state of denial.

If the child's parents are in denial, having other family members in the same state will only prolong the situation for everyone, possibly for a longer period than is beneficial. If the child's parents have reached some level of acceptance, however, the continued denial of other family members can lead to conflict and dispute. In both the examples mentioned above, the family member's statement of denial also contains an implicit accusation of poor parenting, a suggestion that if only the parent did things differently, everything would be perfectly normal. For a parent who knows and has accepted the reality of a child's diagnosis, this type of criticism can be devastating.

The continued denial of an important family member is an issue that many of you will have to confront. If you have reached a stage of at least partial acceptance and your family's reluctance to reach that same outcome is proving to be a problem, you may need to discuss the issue frankly with those concerned. Remember that your family members are in denial precisely because they share your pain, so a gradual, reasoned approach will be far more beneficial than engaging in heated argument.

The Positive Side of Denial

The most important thing to understand about denial in all its forms is that it serves a purpose. Denial is a means by which you can come to terms with your loss, a necessary hurdle on the road to acceptance. Denial helps you to express your grief, and offers some momentary protection from a hostile environment. For those for whom denial is long term or potentially detrimental, professional counseling should be sought. For the most part, however, moving beyond denial is simply a matter of letting nature take its inevitable course.

The most important thing to understand about denial in all forms is that it serves a purpose.

Butt Out of Our Business

Paddy Ryan

I AWAITED THE BIRTH of my first child with a mixture of horror, enthusiasm, and excitement.

My wife, Donna, felt much the same way. We both knew the baby had no gross abnormalities thanks to an amniocentesis done months earlier—a precaution against the higher risks of defects associated with Donna's age.

It had been a model pregnancy. Donna had done all the right things. After an eight-hour labor the baby's head became visible and my heart seemed to stop. Surely it wasn't possible to fit that enormous head through such a narrow gap. My second reaction was, "My God, the baby is hairy!"

And so Emma burst forth and greeted the world with what sounded like a yell of protest. Donna and I did a quick head, limb, and digit count, and when all checked out normal, we began to relax.

Although small, Emma seemed to us to be a perfectly normal baby. The truth was that as new parents neither of us really knew what "normal" was, despite having read all the books. One Friday night, when Emma was around one year old, I was having a quiet drink at my club when a friend approached me.

"I don't know quite how to put this," she said, "but there's something wrong with Emma. I've had two children of my own and she just doesn't seem to be developing normally."

At first I was stunned. Then, to my ultimate shame and chagrin, I told her to "butt out of our business" and insisted that there was nothing wrong with my daughter.

I was really angry because I understood there was some truth in what she said. I also couldn't understand how two "perfect" people—Donna and I—could produce a less than perfect baby. Later, as the truth about Emma unfolded, I was to remember that incident with pain. A true act of friendship, which took considerable courage, was churlishly rejected. I've since apologized.

By the time Emma was three years old, it was apparent she was "different," to say the least. She became very distressed over sounds that didn't bother us at all. She screamed at the noise of workmen cleaning roadside vegetation with weed whackers, and she screamed when the sun shone on her body as she rode in the car. This behavior really annoyed me. I was certain she was acting this way simply to get attention. I reacted by ignoring her distress or asking her to be quiet. What a dumb thing to say to a three-year-old toddler!

Other than those tantalizing hints, Emma's development appeared superficially normal. Her special needs were forcibly brought home to us on the day she started primary school, however. On that first day the teacher had to pry a screaming Emma off my legs. Turning my back and walking away from her was one of the most difficult things I've ever done and still has the capacity to bring tears to my eyes when I think about it.

Going to school was never a pleasure for Emma. Mornings were the worst. Emma would take forever to get dressed. It seemed as if she was deliberately slow so as to be late for class. On several occasions I lost my cool and shouted at her, which only made things worse. It was difficult for me to accept that she had a problem and much easier to believe she was being deliberately obstinate. After all, no child of mine could be less than perfect.

With Emma's condition undiagnosed during her early years of school, my sense of frustration and bewilderment increased. Emma needed remedial teaching, but gaining that specialist help required in part finding some label that could be attached to her behavior. My angry outbursts were also a source of shame, as was the fact that I resented the ridiculous ease with which her younger sister, Kathy, sailed through life. I wanted to take a little from Kathy and give it to Emma.

When Emma was nine and a half, Donna and I separated. At first we all stayed in the same town, and I had regular visits with my daughters. By this time Emma had been easily overtaken both physically and mentally by her younger sister. Donna and I realized that we now had a new problem. Every tiny advance by Emma was greeted with a chorus of praise from the two of us, whereas Kathy's considerable achievements had to reach monumental proportions to even get noticed. In our quest to help Emma we'd produced a chronic overachiever.

Their move to a new city marked the start of better care for Emma. At about this time, I read an eye-opening book about sensory integration dysfunction syndrome. The more I read, the more horrified I became. The book made perfect sense, years too late.

The part that really got to me was the section where the author discussed the ways sensory integration dysfunction syndrome manifests. Mega-guilt trip! I paraphrase, but this is basically what the book said: "Children who take forever to get dressed are not deliberately setting out to try your patience. For them this is an enormously difficult exercise that requires all of their concentration, and completing the activity is truly a major triumph worthy of the utmost praise."

Yes, I did the guilt thing again and wept.

That brings us up-to-date—almost. I've remarried, and recently my wife and I took a trip to Fiji with Emma and Kathy. We tried our hand at ocean kayaking. At first Emma found it totally beyond her and became hugely frustrated. Gentle coaching from my wife slowly produced results, and after half an hour Emma was paddling, albeit badly, but well enough to keep up with us. As her confidence grew, her face changed from one screwed up in concentration to a huge smile. "I'm beating you, Dad," she said as she raced past me.

Six months later I took her kayaking up a river in New Zealand. To my delight and amazement she went almost as far as it was possible to go. During the visit Emma spent two weeks with Kathy, me, and a whole bunch of university students. Watching her interact so positively and perform so well brought a flood of emotion and the dawning realization that against all odds, my ugly ducking was slowly changing into a swan.

I've learned to live with the way that Emma progresses and does things. I've learned to take pride in her accomplishments. I've learned not to feel guilty about the way I used to treat her. I've learned that it isn't a reflection on me that my daughter isn't perfect. I've learned that there is no such thing as perfection anyway. She's changed me, I believe, for the better. There are now times when I wonder who has grown up more over the last fifteen years.

Grandma Knows Best

PAULA ICKES

WHEN YOU'RE A LITTLE GIRL, you most likely want to grow up and become a wife and mother.

You practice nurturing, feeding, and caring for an infant. It's a wonderful feeling when you finally get to experience what you have so often dreamed about, but it comes with mixed emotions. You are happy, nervous, curious, and excited for the child you are about to give life to. You are hopeful that your child will be perfect in every way.

On March 26, 1997, we were blessed with the birth of our daughter, Hannah Renee, the spitting image of perfection. My husband and I were in our glory.

From the first time my grandmother saw Hannah, she was concerned with her hearing. She kept telling me that my baby could not hear. She even thought Hannah had an unusual cry. It just didn't seem normal to her.

Well, keeping in mind that my daughter was perfect, I told Grandma she was crazy. Hannah was fine. But my grandmother didn't give up. For months, every time she saw Hannah, she expressed her concern. Finally, when Hannah was nine months old, we acquiesced and requested a hearing test.

The results were devastating. At the age of one year, Hannah was diagnosed as deaf. Not just deaf, but profoundly deaf. Even hearing aids would be of little use to her.

The diagnosis was overwhelming. I was simply not prepared to hear those words. I figured maybe she had had some fluid in her ears and that inserting some tubes would clear the problem away. Never did I imagine the result we were handed that day.

I came home from the hospital and tried to hide myself away. I didn't want to deal with people. When the pediatrician called to speak to me, I refused to come to the phone. With my bedroom door locked, I sat on my bed all evening asking myself over and over, "Why?" How could this have happened to my child? I kept wondering if I had done something wrong during the pregnancy or if something had happened during delivery.

I came home from the hospital and tried to hide myself away. I didn't want to deal with people.

I thought about all the warnings my grandma had given and how I did not want to accept her advice. She had eight children of her own and thirty grandchildren—I should have listened to her from the beginning! So much for mother knowing best!

After a few days of feeling sorry for my daughter and myself, I slowly came to the realization that she was healthy and that is what was most important. Instead of self-pity I began to adopt a positive attitude, and set about finding out the next step to help my daughter. We were given names of several people to contact who could help us get hearing aids and also start teaching us and Hannah sign language. This was actually an interesting and educational experience.

Hannah began to communicate using sign language. Although I was grateful to be able to "talk" to my daughter, using your hands to communicate with your child is not entirely satisfying. I still felt that she was missing out on so much and that we parents were equally deprived because of the lack of verbal communication.

It was some time after our sign language training began that we were introduced to a procedure called a cochlear implant, a surgically implanted hearing device for the deaf. Although there were few guarantees about how successful the implant would be for Hannah, at the age of two our daughter was fitted with the new technology.

The results have been pleasing. She is now almost five years old and is speaking in a fairly normal manner. Hannah will be mainstreamed into kindergarten next year with other children her age. Believe me, though, the implant certainly hasn't resolved her disability. Hannah cannot wear her device 24/7, yet without it she is completely unable to hear. The implant cannot be worn near water, on the playground, or while she sleeps. If she wakes in the middle of the night, we can't just tell her to go back to sleep. In order for her to know that everything is okay, one of us must get up, turn on a light, and let her see our face.

My family believes Hannah is extremely spoiled, but they don't understand how vulnerable a deaf child is. How could I let her wander around frightened in the middle of a dark night? Hannah is my life and my responsibility; the very least I can do is to make sure she is as comfortable as possible.

The last four years with my daughter have not always been easy, but it has been rewarding in many ways. Life doesn't always deal you a good hand, but what is important is how you play it. Everything moves so fast these days that it is easy to overlook the simple things that make existence precious.

Having a child with a disability makes you slow down and enjoy him or her, perhaps more than most parents whose children are not disabled. I'm not saying I am a better parent, just that I am more appreciative of this little creature of God.

To Sleep, Perchance to Sleep

Doreen Bonnett

It's nearly one in the morning. I just got my son to sleep around midnight. He has sensory integration dysfunction, or DSI. One of his symptoms is insomnia. He can't process sensory input, so he constantly seeks more.

I've always been a night owl, so a son who can't sleep shouldn't be a problem. But I hear these voices telling me I'm a bad mother, I'm too lenient, he needs to know who's boss, blah, blah, blah. They swirl in my head while I lie on top of my hyped-up son, hoping the deep pressure will calm him.

My former therapist says it's okay if Jonathan cries when I hold him because it's a good way for him to release energy. Intellectually I know that, but it's hard to see him in pain. I wind up wired at midnight and perpetually sleep-deprived, like many mothers. I tell myself I'm better because I deal with things most mothers don't. Let's see all those finger waggers cope with DSI. I give them ten minutes, tops.

Emily Kingsley, whose son has Down syndrome, said it was like getting on a plane to Italy and landing in Holland. DSI is like an untracked wilderness—rough terrain, sparsely populated, and mysterious. Most people know very little about it. But people live in the wilderness and some of them enjoy it. I enjoy my son and celebrate his small victories, such as buttoning a button or coloring in the lines.

I keep from beating myself up by harboring visions of better times to come. I imagine Jonathan doing well in school and reading Harry Potter books. It isn't the grand vision most parents have, but I don't have the luxury of taking Harry Potter for granted.

Before Jonathan was diagnosed, I did take things for granted. Odd behavior was just a quirk or a stage he'd grow out of. Potty-training delays were the result of inconsistent methods and too much pressure. It never occurred to me that something might be wrong. Everything I'd read about parenting said that each child is unique and develops at his own pace.

Even when he had a meltdown at preschool and had to be picked up early, I didn't suspect a thing. I chalked it up to a recent trip and a disruption in his routine. Perhaps I was in denial. But I had to do something, so I worked with him for a couple of months, structuring his time. When he got better, I let up a bit. Next thing I knew, he was climbing on tables at preschool. Then one day he bit a friend.

Jonathan became one of more than two thousand children suspended from preschool that year. The thirty-day suspension seemed overly harsh to me. Even people who had accused me of being too permissive agreed. Not even high school students get thirty-day suspensions. I was appalled and distraught because I couldn't take a month off from work to be home with him, but I soldiered on and found him a new preschool.

The transition to the new place was hard, especially since I'd scheduled Jonathan's kindergarten orientation in the middle of the day to accommodate my work schedule. Because of that he missed his nap and got agitated with his teacher. I had to pick him up early because he threw sand and pebbles at her. That's when I realized something was very wrong.

I'd prayed for things to work at the new preschool, so when they didn't, I cursed God. Then I found a developmental and behavioral pediatrician who diagnosed probable DSI. An occupational therapist confirmed it a couple of months later. He's been in therapy weekly for two years as of this September and is making progress.

I'm glad I could afford occupational therapy because the insurance company wouldn't cover it. They only cover therapy for an illness, injury, or surgery. I had to file an appeal to get DSI covered as an illness. It's ridiculous. If I was careless and dropped him on his head, therapy would be covered. But since I'm a good mother merely trying to improve his life, it isn't. My new insurance will cover it, but not 100 percent.

This writing feels jumbled. I could edit it into highly polished prose, but it wouldn't reflect the reality of parenting a child with DSI. The reality is being jumbled, rushing to get your kid to the bus because he didn't fall asleep until midnight and slept late, forgetting his backpack and driving to school to drop it off because he'll have a meltdown without it. Reality is forgetting to breathe.

My husband says I'm a Pollyanna, always looking at the bright side. So, here's the bright side:

There's never a dull moment.

I now truly understand the concept of unconditional love. I wouldn't love my son more if he didn't have DSI and I don't love him less because he does.

I'm blessed with a sweet boy with a terrific laugh, a beautiful smile, and a forgiving soul. I know I'm not the world's greatest mother, but he doesn't.

Recently I spoke with a support-group coordinator and was so relieved to find someone who understands. My goal is to help everyone in Jonathan's life understand and accept him as he is. Sometimes I just want to shout, "People, please, he's only seven."

So many people want Jonathan to fit their image of a good boy that I want to free him from unreasonable expectations. Now if I could just free myself.

Anger

We all boil at different degrees.

RALPH WALDO EMERSON

Introduction

NEIL NICOLL

"IT'S NOT FAIR!" is one of the most common of childhood catchphrases—and little wonder.

In Western society, instilling an appreciation of fairness and justice in young children is considered essential to good parenting. We tell our kids to take turns, to share toys, to be kind and generous to others. Good children are rewarded, bad children punished.

It's hardly surprising, then, that most of us grow up cozy in the unspoken belief that simply being a "good" person will ensure a fairly happy and trouble-free life. Unfortunately this belief in a natural justice, an inherent fairness in life, is not reflected by reality. Just ask the parent of any disabled child.

Bad things happen to good people. The wicked drive Porsches while the kind-hearted catch the bus. Neglectful, even abusive parents are blessed with perfect, healthy children, while loving couples find themselves struggling with a handicapped baby.

Is it any wonder that parents caring for children with disabilities are often overwhelmed by anger and bitterness?

Definition

Anger is one of humanity's strongest and most powerful emotions. Like denial, anger is a natural and automatic response that, in the short term, offers protection from emotional trauma.

Anger arises primarily out of anxiety. Put simply, when we feel anxious, helpless, and overwhelmed by a particular situation, anger comes to the rescue. Not only does it neutralize our anxiety for a while, it can also restore some semblance of power and authority when we need it most.

Understanding Anger

It would be a rare parent indeed who would consciously choose to produce a disabled child. The birth of a special-needs child can turn comfortable lives upside down and place serious strain on even the most solid of family units.

New parents find themselves having to deal with a multitude of emotional upheavals and uncertainties simultaneously. There are medication and therapies to grapple with, school options and respite care to consider, therapists and assessments, hospital visits and support groups. All this baffling new territory must be explored while coming to terms with the stark realization that life has been changed irrevocably.

Sometimes parents may need to move to a different home or change jobs, or forgo interests, ambitions, and friendships in order to be able to meet the needs of their disabled child. They find that their friends no longer call, that a simple restaurant lunch has become a distant dream, and that going to the movies or even taking a short family holiday has become an unworkable logistical nightmare. Many parents begin to feel that they are only able to devote time and energy to their special-needs child at the expense of their other children. This in turn raises their awareness, and anger, at the difficulties associated with obtaining suitable services for a child with a disability—the financial costs, the waiting lists, the lack of options, the official indifference, the essential "unfairness" of it all.

Those without special-needs children will often comment on the apparent strength and patience of such parents. They appear almost "bulletproof," and often attract the admiration of others who feel certain they themselves could not display such resilience under similar circumstances. The truth is that there are no "super parents." It is true that many parents of special-needs children have developed great determination and superb coping skills. But if you were to ask them about it, they would tell you almost unanimously that this was not what they wanted. They would tell you these perceptions are all illusion. Parents of children with disabilities simply have to work harder and be more patient and give up more of themselves. And that is not fair, nor is it understood, valued, or acknowledged.

Parents of children with disabilities simply have to work harder and be more patient and give up more of themselves.

Displacement

If you've ever kicked your desk after getting yelled at by your boss, or snapped at your husband because you accidentally burned dinner, then you've experienced displacement.

One of the "side effects" of anger, displacement occurs when we shift the focus of our anger from its original target onto an object or person less threatening or more convenient than the original source.

For parents of special-needs children, displacement is a common phenomenon. The real source of their anxiety—their child and the child's disability—is too painful to face, so other, more accessible targets are found. Some parents enter into protracted and emotional disputes with service providers such as school or medical specialists. They may become overzealous in their attempts to "save" their child, insisting on the impossible from specialist support or setting impossible goals for the child's teacher to achieve.

While such behaviors may appear irrational at times, from a psychological point of view it is not merely wasted energy. It is important that parents feel they are doing all they can for their child, just as it is vital that they occasionally externalize their feelings of guilt and anger onto others, to stop blaming themselves for a moment and let others carry the burden for a time.

Service agencies and other professionals can find parental anger quite challenging and intimidating, usually because they don't understand its source. An angry parent yelling at a teacher may not really bear any malice toward their victim, but simply be displacing their grief and disappointment onto whoever happens to be handy at the time.

Another common approach taken by angry parents is to choose care or treatment options not recommended by the professionals and to become outraged when a usually understanding doctor or teacher refuses to offer any assistance with an untried or "radical" approach. While understanding the need for service providers to maintain their professional integrity, it is also important for them to sometimes allow parents the dignity of failure—on their own terms.

Dealing with Anger

For most people, anger is a transient state. A traffic jam, a TV with bad reception, an argument with your spouse, a check that bounces—all are common and legitimate causes of anger. But when the traffic frees up, the TV is repaired, your partner forgives you, and you finally get your finances in order, the anger vanishes and is quickly forgotten. Parents with special-needs children aren't so fortunate. They are faced with a real and inescapable problem for which there is no quick fix.

Rather than try to continue to fix what cannot be repaired, parents wishing to deal with their anger in a constructive way need to remember the following points:

Whenever possible, concentrate on how you handle the problem of your child's disability rather than trying to constantly find a solution. Acknowledge that there are some things over which you have no control and strive instead to do the very best you can with those areas you can influence.

If you feel too filled with rage to express yourself appropriately, retreat and find a safer way to vent your rage. Punch a pillow, write down your anger on paper, phone a friend.

Try relaxation therapies such as yoga and deep-breathing exercises. Practice these daily or when time permits.

Avoid using negative words such as *never* and *always* when talking to others. Statements such as "You never give Sam a chance to speak in class" or "Why are you never home when I need help with the kids?" just allow you to justify your anger and increase your level of hostility.

Before you give in fully to your anger, try fending it off with a little logic. Anger is generally an illogical emotion, and a little clear-headed thinking can sometimes quell its intensity. Tell yourself that the world/your daughter's teacher/your husband/your mother-in-law, and so on are not really out to make your life difficult.

It is incredibly important that you take good care of yourself physically, emotionally, and mentally. As unpalatable as it may seem to some parents, irregular breaks through respite care are vital circuit breakers. They give you time to devote to yourself and to other family members. Some service providers are able to offer parents special "pamper" days when the parents can become the focus of loving attention for a little while.

Support groups can be of immense benefit. Talking about your problems and fears with others who understand can be truly liberating.

Why Should It Matter?

SHERRIE BALL

LAST NIGHT I'D HAD IT! All I needed to hear was another up-date on our son, Braden's, health come spewing from my hus-band, Steve's, mouth when the man clearly had no clue.

"So-and-so asked me how Braden was doing and I said he was fine, doing great!" He continued: "I said he'd had a stomach thing that made him sick once, but now it's gone and he eats normally."

Every night the same routine! My husband comments on how great Braden is doing, pointing out every deed as though I wear blinders all day and don't realize how unusually sharp Braden was. Predictably, he sits down to eat with Braden on his lap and, when he's finished, remarks on how Braden ate a whole cow and half a hog for supper. "Haven't you fed him all day?" is Steve's usual remark at the end of mealtime.

Anger, hatred, resentment, and even jealousy creep under my collar. "How dare he presume to tell anyone how Braden is?" I wonder. Finally, I inquire with venom on my tongue, "How exactly would you have any idea how he is since you don't even ask me about any of his clinic visits?"

Anger, hatred, resentment, and even jealousy creep under my collar.

I was incredulous at the fact that Steven thought Braden wasn't even using his gastrostomy tube anymore when in fact he receives 75 percent of his nutrition through it. How is it, I wonder, that he can be so "Lucy in the Sky" blind?

My life since Braden's birth has revolved around his health, or lack of it. All of my other children have been forced to adjust to it as well. My three older children accompany me to the university clinics, and have stayed at the Ronald McDonald House or hotels near the hospital. They are all accustomed to Braden's therapist or visiting nurses as they come in and out of our lives. They participate with his tube feedings, and the eldest has even been allowed to stay at our local hospital with Braden. We have all trudged to the local doctor's office and pharmacies innumerable times.

Somehow it appears that I have allowed my husband to blissfully escape the commotion that has changed every aspect of the rest of the household. As I type, I wonder if I have allowed him this retreat, or if he has chosen to bunker in a hole himself.

Braden goes regularly to an orthopedic clinic, genetic clinic, neurology clinic, gastroenterology clinic, disability clinic, and nutritionist, as well as our local doctors and other services out of the home. How can all this proceed unnoticed? How can Steven not have realized that I quit college and took a leave of absence from my volunteer work? Surely he must have noticed that Braden occupies the space in our bed that he himself once occupied?

What other dimension does he exist in? Doesn't he see me slapping away at the computer keyboard searching the Internet for medical works that might contain definitions of terminology that are out of my grasp or answers left by the doctors for me to sort out? Surely he has observed at least one of my notebooks filled with Braden's intake/outtake records, or the vast folder jammed with worksheets? Perhaps the mountainous pile of insurance statements bulging out of the mail organizer has caught his eye, or the bulletin board in our kitchen that I keep to track Braden's revolving schedule. Haven't all the cardboard boxes given him a hint that the courier stops weekly to deliver supplies? I suppose it wouldn't be unreasonable, then, for him to know that I have spent hours on the telephone with suppliers, nurses, doctors, various schedulers, Social Security offices, social service agencies, school personnel, pharmacies, and a multitude of other "significant" groups now involved in my life.

Does Steven have any concept of how much money has been disbursed for Braden's care or have any inkling of how much will be expended in his future? Could he possibly know just how many times I have gathered up our financial records to elicit support any way I can? Measureless!

Admittedly I am angry that I have always had to be the one compelled to grip my son's arm for the lab, to pin him down for the frequent IV pokes, to withdraw his food, to assist with the insertion of his nasogastric tube, to support his gastrostomy feedings, to dose his medications, and to stay awake endless nights at the hospital. I resent that I alone am left to sift through his volumes of medical records. I don't appreciate being the person to escort him through the legions of medical tests, surgeries, and procedures. I loathe having to hold him down while he's being administered anesthesia. I fear.

I do not like that my husband seems compelled to "beef up" our son to me. It feels as though he can't simply appreciate him for being the special child that he is. It makes me sense that he feels our son has to be normal to be of value. I tried recently to explain microcephaly to Steve and he bristled, "He's not retarded!"

"No, he's not," I say, and continue trying to explain Braden's expected potential as it was explained to me by the neurologist. Inwardly I think, "So, what if he was? Would it make him any less deserving of affection?"

Does he have to meet some median IQ to be of value? Are you embarrassed? Does his genetic abnormality somehow cut into your self-image? I seethe. I contemplate my role in all this. Have I, in my zest to ensure that I do everything possible for Braden's future, taken over? Has my own requirement to ensure that all the trash is in order made the garbage pile a bit too tidy?

Has my very own self-assurance made everything appear to be ordinary in our lives and with our son? Have I been the one to allow my husband to continue to sail the placid waters while I raft through the churning rapids alone?

I ask myself if I am truly jealous of his ignorant nirvana or simply indignant because I perceive that if he doesn't understand the distance I've traveled with Braden, then he can't appreciate all that I've sacrificed of myself?

Why should it matter? I realize it shouldn't hold any value whatsoever. What my husband chooses to believe or acknowledge shouldn't matter if it doesn't hurt Braden. I know Steven is devoted to our son. They love each other, and in Braden's world that is what matters most. I know in my heart I will continue to pursue that which is best not only for Braden but for all my children.

I know I need to cast aside the anger, the resentment, the hatred, and the jealousy. I've admitted it exists, that's a first step.

Willing to Learn

KATHY WINTERS

I HAD NO IDEA what I was in for when I decided to become a mother. At that time, if someone had warned me of what lay ahead, I would surely have opted for a childless existence, lavishing my maternal instincts on a couple of furry pets.

I can almost hear the conversation:

"So, you'd like to know what your future children will be like? Well, let's just take a peek, then . . . oh dear!

"It appears that your first two children are going to be quite complex and challenging little people! The oldest will be intelligent, responsible, and sensitive. He'll be gifted in math and science. He'll have hands that can skillfully weave yarn into cloth, mold clay into beautiful figures, and draw three-dimensional forms with amazing accuracy!

"But those same hands will struggle to button shirts, snap pants, hold a pencil, and write a sentence. He'll be isolated from his peers by an inability to remember faces, a learning disability in reading and writing, and delays in fine and gross motor skills. His problems, being subtle, will go unnoticed for a while as he struggles to compensate for them. But his stress will show in his behavior. He'll be a perfectionist, a loner, anxious at school, and belligerent with his teachers.

"Your second son will have a smile that lights up the room, eyes that melt your heart, and a delightful sense of humor. He'll have a quick mind, a compassionate outlook, and he'll love to sing. However, he'll also be an emotionally volatile child, given to angry outbursts whenever things don't go his way. He'll easily become bored and frustrated and will express his discontent loudly, especially in public. He'll be careless, impulsive, fidgety, and disorganized. His behavior will eventually lead to diagnoses of ADHD and Tourette's syndrome.

"And it seems that both your sons will have sensory integration dysfunction. Of course, the world being what it is, and neurological conditions such as theirs being difficult to diagnose and controversial among professionals and laypeople alike, you will often be blamed for their behavior. It will be a rough journey filled with chaos, sadness, guilt, fear, anger, and confusion. Much of it you will have to go alone as your husband buries his feelings in denial, and friends and family either turn away or criticize. You don't have to take this journey, but if you do, it will be worth it in the end. For if you travel with an open heart, you will receive wonderful gifts along the way."

Wonderful gifts? Where are there gifts in this? Many days I can't see them and I wish that someone had warned me ahead of time and given me the option to say no. But no one warned me. Life isn't like that. Whether by cosmic design or because of a random toss of the gene-pool dice, these are my children . . . and I adore them.

But I also often feel overwhelmed, angry, and fearful for the future. I envy those for whom parenting seems so much simpler, while at the same time feeling guilty for my anger and envy. For I know that many parents have children with much more devastating disabilities than mine. So what right do I have to envy others? How can I feel angry and resentful? Perhaps because my sons' disabilities are hidden, *I envy those for whom parenting seems so much simpler, while at the same time feeling guilty for my anger and envy.* complex, and misunderstood. So instead of support I get judgment. Instead of help I get criticism. Instead of answers I get more questions.

But I do know that there are gifts in this. Sometimes weeks, even months, go by where I can't see them. And then suddenly, out of the blue, one will appear. They arrive in the form of my personal growth. There's my greater confidence and assertiveness, molded through years of advocating for my sons in a system that puts money ahead of people. There's the greater understanding that I have gained of what unconditional love really is as I've learned to love my children even when their behavior reflects badly on me as their mother. Then there's the gift of my newfound compassion for children with hidden disabilities, my desire to help them, and the joy I feel in using all my hard-earned knowledge to guide another parent through the complex maze of his or her own journey. These are but a few of the gifts I have received from my special children.

Yes, in rare and precious moments I see the gifts quite clearly. I see that my children are my teacher, the lessons coming in ever-changing forms as they grow and we face new challenges. And the tests are the way I respond to those challenges. When I learn the lessons and pass the tests, I receive the gifts.

Some of the tests I have not yet passed. There's the test of patience. What a gift it will be if I can only learn that one. There's trust and acceptance. You may have noticed that I still struggle with those. Gratitude—will I ever reach a point when I can look back at these years and say, without reservation, that I'm grateful for my children's problems, for they were the means through which life's gifts were delivered to me? I don't know—maybe. But, in the meantime, I'm just grateful that I wasn't given the choice.

When I look into my children's eyes, when I see them smile, when they make me laugh, when I watch them sharing their talents with the world, then I know that they are so very special. They were meant to be here—exactly as they are. But I would never have willingly chosen to have them if I'd known of the struggles we would face. I didn't have a choice in my children's disabilities. But I do have the choice to grow from the experience, to be willing to learn the lessons that parenting them offers.

I'm usually willing. But, and God forgive me, some days I just want to feel angry.

The Why of It

Michelle Portman

Men do not think they know a thing till they have
grasped the why of it.

ARISTOTLE, Physics

RAGE. That is what I felt when my daughter was born with
half her head deformed, including the entire right hemisphere
of her brain. Seething rage. The birth and in fact the whole
pregnancy had been long and hard. As time went on, it might
have been easier if all I felt was rage, but soon I felt deep depression, sadness, and fear as well. Among that confusion of
feeling, a relentless anger flashed in the background, fueled by
questions.

When I was still in the hospital, right after the first suspicions
were raised because of our daughter's huge right ear and cheek,
my first thought was, "Do I have to go through raising a disabled
child too?" I was tired. Tired of life, tired of overcoming adversity,
exhausted from years of disappointing circumstances. It was a
desperate question. I don't even know who I was asking. I am not
a religious person. Somehow, though, I knew the answer was yes,
I would have to raise a disabled child.

My daughter has epidermal nevus syndrome, a very rare condition that can affect any part or all of the body. The skin of the affected part is abnormal and looks like a huge, raised birthmark. In
my daughter the affected side of her head also grows faster and
larger than normal, including the facial muscles, skull, jaw, teeth—

everything. The worst of it is that her brain is affected too, one side being completely enlarged and malformed.

My first child, a healthy boy, was three when my first husband left me. I had always wanted two children, but his leaving precluded that option for many years. I was almost forty years old when I met my second husband after six years of being single.

When one asks, "Why?" the question "How?" is never far off. So it was with me. I couldn't understand how Ella could have been born with such a rare condition. Of course, it wasn't just the physical deformity but the illness she suffered that tormented me—mainly debilitating seizures since the time she was two weeks old until she had a hemispherectomy operation at ten months, an operation in which the entire abnormal half of the brain is taken out.

I feared for my daughter's health and her future, but I also feared for my marriage. I worried that Etan would reject me. My first husband had had a fit when I announced my pregnancy ten years earlier. When my son was two weeks old, we had a fight that almost cost me my life when, for the first and only time, he physically abused me. He was determined not to give up a thing in his life for our son. Three years after that he left me for another woman nine years my junior.

To my surprise, things with Etan were immediately different. Despite all the heartbreak we both experienced upon the birth of Ella, he never swayed from his dedication to both her and me. One day upon returning home from a week in the hospital with Ella drugged up to the hilt on seizure medication, in a very tender way he told me how much he needed me. He also helped me let go and move on. I realized, through watching his example, that the searching questions of why and how would not help us much, and I slowly left them by the wayside.

A lot of loss comes with giving birth to a child with severe medical needs. However, this loss paled in comparison to some of the other losses I've known in my life. The loss of childhood, losses that came from growing up in a dysfunctional family, business loss. Let's face it: life is loss. Sure, I get tired of facing the missed milestones in Ella's development, of the endless doctors appointments, of the constant anxiety of seeing another damaging seizure. But by the time Ella came into my life, I was in a different place.

The day Ella had the brain surgery that her neurologists recommended as the only hope for her to live without uncontrollable seizures was a day that proved that to me. I vividly remember how we passed our smiling Ella into the arms of the anesthesiologist. About seven hours into the operation, a nurse came to speak to us. We had seen families come and go all that day. Entire dramas had unfolded. We were the only family who had been there since the beginning of the day. Every two hours we had received updates. This time, however, the nurse sat down with us. She said they couldn't stop Ella's bleeding and that it was a critical point in the operation. Because of the abnormal structure of Ella's head, the surgeons had run into unexpected physiology, and Ella was in grave danger.

I didn't know what to think. Again, as with Ella's birth, I stared blankly in disbelief, not knowing even what to hope for. I turned and saw the strain on Etan's face. Each wrinkle in his skin seemed suddenly deeper, and I saw tears well up in his eyes as he began to cry. Through all my confusion I knew then that I was not alone. It was a new feeling for me. I comforted Etan as I fought down a big lump in my throat.

Ella made it through the hemispherectomy after being administered a record amount of blood. Recovery will take a long time, and Ella will always have some cognitive and physical disability, although it's unclear how much. That takes a long time to accept—longer than Ella's recovery from life-threatening surgery, which has, at least up to the time of this writing, cured her seizure disorder. But I see now how Ella's condition has brought me to view our family as a stronger, often better unit whose members will always support one another. Not every family or even every couple has that.

Don't get me wrong. I hate that saying "God only gives you what you can handle." Or "special children for special parents." I don't want to be special or heroic! I wouldn't have chosen that for a second. But then, I didn't choose. I did learn to trust myself and maybe to trust in fate. If nothing else, I learned to forgive fate and appreciate what I do have.

A "Perfect" Family

Nancy Archer

Considered high-risk due to my age and complications from my previous pregnancy, I opted for an amniocentesis, solely for peace of mind.

The results were normal and confirmed what we had suspected: we were having a little boy. When our son was born, healthy and beautiful with a full head of blond hair, our "perfect" little family seemed complete.

At first, baby Joey did everything expected of him. He ate well, slept well (except when we wanted him to!), and otherwise did all the usual baby things. I did notice that he did not look directly at me but rather toward the side or top of my head. Not giving it too much thought, I brought it up at his two-month checkup.

The pediatrician spent forty-five minutes attempting to get Joey to focus on a light, a toy, on anything. Not getting a response, she immediately sent us to a pediatric ophthalmologist. This specialist examined Joey, my husband, and me before finally speaking.

"I think you know what I'm going to say," she said gently. We had no idea.

"Well, no, that's why we're here." Brilliant!

"Joey has a form of albinism." We stared blankly at her.

"Alba— . . . what?"

"He's an albino. He has no pigment in the back of his eye and his eyesight is extremely poor. He may end up with 'getting around' vision, but he could also be legally blind."

"But he looks perfectly normal to us!"

He did look perfectly normal to us, as my husband and I are both very fair and our daughter has platinum blond hair. But Joey couldn't see. Our beautiful baby boy couldn't see us. We were devastated.

I do not know how I made it home that afternoon after his appointment. I couldn't see for the tears. How could this happen to us? Shock was quickly followed by guilt. I was sure that God was punishing me for some past infraction.

Then the anger set in. Anger at God, anger at the world, and anger at all the future teasing Joey may receive from his peers. How would he do in school? Would the other kids make fun of him? Would he be able to drive? Would he ever see us and know us as his parents who love him and want the best for him? I wanted answers to these and other questions. But that day all I could do was go home and hold him and hold him, never putting him down even when he protested.

The following day at my mothers' group, a question was raised. What would you change about your child if you could? "Changing diapers," said one mother. "Sleepless nights," said another. I felt so alone then in my pain and so angry with the other moms. I would gladly change diapers and get up all night long for the rest of my life if only my son could have his vision. I left, vowing never to return to the group, as they were obviously a bunch of ninnies.

After another day of anger and crying, I realized I had to do something positive. Something for Joey, and something for me. So I started the long road of research into his condition and any possible treatments. I signed up for every piece of information I could get and read every Web posting from parents just like us.

After another day of anger and crying, I realized I had to do something positive.

The very first thing I discovered is that it is not considered politically correct to refer to people like Joey as "albinos." They are "persons with albinism." This "person first" attitude is also true of other disabilities. What an epiphany for me! What had seemed a distant problem for others became a distinct reality for me at that moment. Joey was a person—a son and a brother—first and foremost. I vowed I would treat him as much as possible as if he were normal. No more endlessly holding him, hour after hour.

The next important thing I discovered from my research was that I was not alone. One day, while reading Web postings, I came across a woman who had a little girl only a week older than Joey. As a parent, she was experiencing all the same despair and anxiety we had. Since our children are so close in age, we became e-mail pals and provide each other with support and someone to whom to vent if need be.

Joey's diagnosis has changed many things for me. I feel I am a more patient and caring parent and person. It still breaks my heart when he hears me but can't see me. But when I am close enough and he does see me . . . wow, the smile and laughter he has for me makes my day!

I also feel I am now more open to other people. When we all go out, especially as a family, we are told how beautiful our children are and we are asked where they can get some of those cool sunglasses for their child. Sometimes I explain what they are for and sometimes I just smile and thank them for the compliment. In this way I met someone in the airport who also had a child with albinism. I eventually returned to the mothers' group and discovered that they were a group of caring individuals, willing to help out in any way possible.

I hope that Joey gets all the normal things a young boy, and later a young man, wants. I hope he grows up not dwelling on his differences but focusing on what he can accomplish. And I will be there for him, advocating and encouraging, but hopefully not smothering. It's hard to go to college if your mother insists on holding you twenty-four hours a day!

I still don't have all the answers to all my questions. But I do know that I am not alone and that there are wonderful organizations and programs that can help him live as normal a life as possible. Joey may not be able to play football like his dad did, and he may not be able to drive a car, but there are many other things he may be able to do.

We have his whole life ahead to discover these things together.

Why Me?

RAYLENE SMITH

I CAN'T DO a damn thing to ease the pain except to try to hug him, try to hold his hand, try to smile for him.

I tell myself that there are millions of people in the world far worse off than him—but this is happening to my son and I hate it. I try to stifle my hurt feelings when he physically pushes me away saying, "I'm not a kid, Mom"—the teenage mantra. But he is a kid—my kid—and I know that deep down he really wants that hug when he feels so ill. I hate his stoicism.

Rationally—if one can be rational in such circumstances—I know that it's his way of coping. I hate that too. How can he be so accepting when I'm so angry? Rejection by someone you love so deeply is the ultimate humiliation. I would sacrifice a limb or even a marriage to take away my son's pain, that is, in part, my pain too. It hurts so much, I sometimes find myself having to make a quick escape to the bathroom so he won't see my tears. I feel so foolish.

I constantly ask—of whom I don't know—"Why my child? What did I do that was so bad that the reprisals were not on me but on my beautiful baby?" There had been something wrong with my son from the very beginning, and I thought that that first surgery would be the end of it. How naive! Handing over my sleeping baby to a surgical nurse was quite possibly the single most dreadful action I have ever performed. I turned away and sobbed in a huge, chest-heaving motion, thinking I would never catch my breath again. I was so frightened he wouldn't be returned to me.

I hate that the world-at-large sometimes appears immune to

the feelings of sick and disabled people. I want to kick the teacher who once made an incredibly ignorant comment about the way my son looks, yell at the person who unsuccessfully attempted to conceal a look of almost-horror at my poor emaciated child, strangle the girl who commented loudly about his stature and asked how old he was—in a room full of people. But, mostly, I want to scream: "Mind your own business! Keep your comments to yourself! He's a beautiful person. Look at the inside, not the outside." And most of all: "Think first and please don't say something that will hurt his feelings, and mine."

I go to work for several reasons, one of which is to be able to think about things other than my child's problems and my fears for him. Until very recently I thought I was the only one who needed help to deal with my family problems. Why me? Three out of five of my immediate family are not well people, two with specific chronic diseases. It's just not fair! How come it's always me who picks up the pieces, runs interference for them, is a slave to them all? They didn't warn me about this in Marriage 101. And they didn't tell me how to save myself. Life is a constant learning curve, but I must be stuck somewhere in the middle.

"God never gives us more than we can cope with," or so the saying goes. I have grave doubts. I believe in religious tradition and I like the warm feeling of being in a place of religious devoutness. But the act of participation in a church service seems to trigger off an emotional war within me. Who wrote these fairytales? I find myself thinking. I recite the words, but they don't mean anything to me. I couldn't care less. Why are "things sent to try us"? Why would God, if there is one, allow so much madness in the world? Enough is enough. I don't want to be tried anymore!

It feels very good to get all this out of me. Very cathartic. I hadn't realized I was still so angry at the world. I prefer to think of myself as just a fun-loving, youthful-thinking wife and mother— not a person who happens to have a sick child. Big deal! I cope. The face I present to the world is one of happiness and satisfaction with my lot.

Interesting how multifaceted the human condition really is.

Difficult Journeys

Michelle Markle

PEOPLE SAY THAT children change your life forever. When one of your children has a disability, this sentiment sounds like a gross understatement.

With the birth of my daughter, Kiley, there began the most life-changing and challenging journey I've ever experienced. Her multiple disabilities have taken me out of a life where I'd achieved comfort, success, independence, and some certainty about my coping abilities, and plunged me into a world of chaos, hospitalizations, orthotics, therapies, surgeries, anger, and grief.

Until that point in my life I had never known ongoing sadness. Nor had I experienced such a vast array of other emotions—anger, loss, and disappointment. The disappointment encircles lost dreams—of things that I had hoped for my daughter, for myself, for my son, and for my husband. Such lofty things as a relationship with her where she talks and she tells me what she feels and wants; lunches where we chat and dream.

And then there are the simple things I had hoped for, and simply expected of, her. Such basic things as sleeping in a normal pattern, speaking, getting dressed, and feeding herself. My sadness is about seeing her sheer outward beauty and wondering how a child so absolutely beautiful cannot move fluidly, see birds flying in the air, or learn at the rate most others do.

The anger is about things not turning out the way I'd imagined. I am angry with caretakers and community settings who exclude my daughter because her behavior doesn't fit their mold or standards. I am angry with physicians who are rude, avoid tough questions, and have no bedside manner. I sometimes feel wrath and place unwarranted blame on my husband for talking me into having another child, and anger with myself for agreeing. And I feel indignation at the past and future challenges Kiley's disabilities impose, along with feeling the loss of opportunities that can never eventuate in our lives.

Although I had had a miserable pregnancy wrought by constant illness, nausea, and insomnia, there were no medical indications that Kiley had any abnormalities. I was assured, after two sonograms, that her brain and other structures were forming properly. All the while, however, I had an ominous feeling that the child I was carrying was not okay.

Shortly after Kiley's birth, I became acutely aware that something was wrong; her body was like a rag doll with little muscle tone, her sucking reflex was impaired, and she just looked unhealthy. I remember hoping her lethargy was a side effect of the epidural I had received during the long, fourteen-hour delivery. But her continued unresponsiveness in the following weeks and months validated my worst fears. I had a child with disabilities.

The next six months were spent trying to calm her continuous crying. They were also spent in the hospital, fighting for her life. It was during these months that I recall selfishly wishing she would die so that life would not be so hard. Kiley was not what I had "ordered." She didn't fit my ideal of a daughter or a playmate for my son. I feared the changes that would have to be made in order to care for her, and I feared above all else that I would not be able to love her.

I feared above all else that I would not be able to love her.

My life changed abruptly from the day of Kiley's birth. From contentment I had been thrust into a life of fear, distress, unrelenting fatigue, and intense remorse for having a child who required so much of my time, energy, and money. The dreams and goals I had in place in my life had been seriously thwarted. I questioned why God would let such a thing occur. I certainly didn't feel equipped to handle this enormous task. Was this a punishment or his testing of me to see if I would pass or fail? In the course of grappling with my intense feelings, I learned that questions like these make people uncomfortable. I have found that Kiley's disability and particularly my feelings about her disability have alienated family members and long-term friends. I have also become wary of sharing my situation with new acquaintances.

I cannot deny that parenting Kiley has been an arduous task for me. I have already known the joy of motherhood, yet this joy was absent with Kiley. There is no joy in caring for an inconsolable, wailing child who was not able to suck, respond visually, or stay asleep for more than two hours at a time for the first two and a half years of her life. Instead of enjoying my beautiful baby girl, instead of nursing and bonding with her, I felt intense anger, dread, and sadness. There is an emptiness in me that so much wants to experience the typical things that a mother expects in a relationship with her child. There is also a bitterness that I wish did not exist. At times I have felt as though my heart and my head were disjointed.

Kiley has taught me countless truths about myself and about life. Many of the truths about myself I would have preferred not to know. I have come to realize how utterly selfish I was and how omnipotent I believed I was. Kiley's disabilities have shown me that the small irritations of life are nothing to worry about anymore. Kiley has taught me that the things in life that were once important to me have a different value. Not that my values are unimportant, but rather, my life plans have been shifted, interrupted for now. My dreams are much less lofty than before, my life goals much simpler. The demands of caring for Kiley have taught me how constant stress has adversely affected my health and how much harder I must work at taking care of myself. She has taught me how to love her in any condition. But all these truths, all this knowledge has not come without an abundance of tears.

Currently, at the age of four, my dear Kiley now imitates simple things such as laughing and basic gross motor movements such as waving good-bye. Many of the vocalizations she is beginning to make are meaningless to the world. But as her mom, they are joyful utterances to me. And yet, at other times, I am saddened by her uncommon simplicity. I am aware that the thoughts I once had that she would die are part of the grief cycle that was necessary to pass through. I believe sleep deprivation certainly played a large part in my difficult adjustment to her disabilities, as did grief. Even now I continue to grapple with grief. I do not like being sad, and it remains a struggle for me to rediscover the joy in life. Usually an optimist, I feel that some days I am regarded by my friends and family as an intense drag.

Despite my best efforts in trying to describe to others what parenting a disabled child is like, I have come to learn that parents with children who are developing normally cannot know what every waking hour is like for those of us with a disabled child. I have been called a martyr. While I did choose to have another child, I certainly did not choose to have a child who is emotionally and physically incapacitated. I'm no martyr. I am simply Kiley's mom under very straining circumstances. My old, comfortable life is no longer a reality. Missed opportunities have been devastating to me, and I am sad and at times angry about these losses.

Caring for Kiley has been the most physically and emotionally exhausting job I've ever had. The journey has been long and often unrewarding. And it's far from over. Only God can know the heartache intermixed with joy that I continue to experience daily with Kiley. It's true that I have come a long way toward healing, toward embracing her abilities and inabilities. I now know I can endure the task that is set before me. Yet still, I must often remind myself of this fact—especially on difficult days when I am overly fatigued or unable to understand Kiley's needs.

My message to you is that you're not alone in your journey, your feelings are very real, and your task of parenting is extraordinarily difficult. If you're the parent of a special-needs child, then we speak the same language, and my heart goes out to you.

Depression

If depression is creeping up and must be faced,
learn something about the nature of the beast.
You may escape without a mauling.

DR. R. W. SHEPHERD, 1978

Introduction

NEIL NICOLL

I T'S BEEN DESCRIBED AS THE "BLACK DOG," the "hidden menace," and the "secret sadness." It has been the personal scourge of some of history's most famous and infamous players: from Alexander the Great and Napoleon through to Edgar Allan Poe, Ernest Hemingway, and singer Janis Joplin.

Depression is one of the most common mental health problems in the world, and yet remains largely underestimated and sadly misunderstood by many. For the parents of disabled children, depression can present a constant and very real threat.

Definition

Depression is best defined as a prolonged feeling of intense sadness, often accompanied by associated feelings of worthlessness, inadequacy, and lethargy. Both sadness and depression are perfectly normal and understandable reactions to grief and loss, trauma and shock. Those coming to terms with the birth of a disabled child should be conscious of the fact that depression can occur at any stage of the grieving process.

Symptoms

The most common symptoms associated with depression include:

- Sadness, often acute
- Irritability
- Feelings of hopelessness
- A sense that life's pleasures are no longer enjoyable

- Crying and weeping, sometimes uncontrollably
- Sleep difficulties
- Lethargy
- Reduced sex drive
- Somatic complaints, such as headaches, digestive problems, and various unexplained aches and pains
- Appetite loss or significant change in appetite
- Increased consumption of alcohol and other drugs
- Suicidal thoughts or, in extreme cases, attempts

At some stage of our lives, we will all probably feel a little depressed. Feeling blue over a job loss, a failed relationship, or financial difficulties isn't necessarily a sign of an ongoing clinical problem. It is important to differentiate between reasonable feelings of sadness and actual clinical depression.

As a general rule, a diagnosis of unipolar major depression (or major depressive disorder) would only be made if a person was found to have five or more of the above symptoms, and to be impaired in their everyday functioning by those symptoms, for a period of at least two months.

Acceptable feelings of sadness and depression are usually transitory—a reaction to a specific incident that has been difficult to come to terms with. In time the feeling passes as we regain our equilibrium and sense of well-being and begin to function as we had before the crisis or trauma occurred.

Clinical depression, on the other hand, is a more chronic state of being and is far less likely to be resolved without specific interventions such as therapy or medication.

Depression Triggers

Parents of disabled children may experience sadness and depression for many reasons: the realization that their hopes and expectations for their child have not been met, the loss of the child they wanted and hoped for, the understanding that their lives have been irreversibly changed and that they are not fully in control of the events occurring around them. Sometimes depression in such circumstances has an additional physical component born of fatigue and worry.

Depression can also arise, or be triggered by, very specific issues. As a parent, you may feel you are coping very well, are emotionally strong, and have come to terms with the implications of your child's disability. Then something as simple as an unkind comment from a member of the public or a bad day at school is enough to bring back a flood of negative emotions and possibly feelings of depression.

Parents of children with disabilities are just as prone to depression as are people grieving the loss of a loved one, with a number of significant differences:

- Whereas death brings a degree of closure, those with disabled children are faced every day with the source of their pain. The physical presence of a very much alive child may exacerbate and prolong depressive episodes.
- Parents often have little or no time to grieve and heal. They often need to be "functional" almost immediately to meet the huge demands of their child. This unresolved sadness may have far-reaching consequences. Conversely, some parents report being glad to be so busy with their child. They believe it gives them something positive to work toward and perhaps distracts them from falling into greater despair.

Fear of becoming depressed is often a major source of anxiety and depression in itself. Parents fear that if they fall into depression, their child may not receive the care he or she requires. Some also worry about what a depressive episode would say about their ability to cope and their parental skills.

Dealing with Depression

If you suspect you may be suffering from depression, it is vital that you discuss the matter with your partner or other trusted loved one, openly, honestly, and as soon as possible. You need to receive acknowledgment about how difficult your role can be, and to be reassured that you do not need to be a "super parent" every day of the year. Try to speak freely about your feelings and reactions to some of the everyday problems you encounter. Don't feel that your sadness is a secret burden that you must carry silently. Martyrdom is not a prerequisite of good parenthood.

Similarly, if you feel your partner may be heading toward depression, encourage them to speak about their feelings and try to be as supportive as possible at all times. Keeping open lines of communication within the context of a busy and perhaps rather stressful household is no easy feat, but it is something that should be strived for nevertheless.

Treatment for depression generally falls into three main categories.

- Antidepressant medications. There are a vast number of medications available, with the most popular being selective serotonin reuptake inhibitors (SSRIs). Many of these drugs are very effective and usually have minimal side effects. Your doctor is the best source for information and advice on this matter.
- Psychotherapy, particularly cognitive-behavioral therapy and interpersonal therapy. While some people may require individual sessions with a psychologist, therapy can also take the form of support groups, Internet chat rooms, and regular chats with an understanding friend. Parent support groups offer the chance to share your feelings with others in the same circumstance, and can be particularly beneficial to those suffering depression. Research from the U.S.-based Depression and Related Affective Disorders Association (DRADA) reveals that 80 percent of people with depression improved when they received either medication or psychotherapy, or a combination of both.
- Herbal remedies. These have become increasingly popular in recent years for a wide range of ailments, including depression.

Don't Always Trust the "Experts"

MARGARET HENC

OUR FIRST CHILD, a son, was born in 1984. From the beginning he was unsettled and couldn't seem to stay asleep, no matter what I tried and whose advice I took. My son could only be consoled by being constantly held or rocked—if I put him down awake, he would cry hysterically. Getting the most basic things done involved a choice between holding him or leaving him to cry, which I had to do at times.

Before long I was exhausted and discouraged. I felt I was failing somehow. As we had no practical support, I also felt very isolated. Beneath all those emotions lurked a growing concern that something just wasn't right with my child. Constantly jumpy and tense, my son would gag at any food that wasn't completely smooth in texture, and yet happily sit eating dirt and sand at every opportunity.

At nine months he started walking and quickly progressed to emptying out the fridge and cupboards, relentlessly playing in and with water, climbing furniture, sitting in boxes and banging saucepans—always by himself. When he was quiet, I would find him staring at the flickering lights on our stereo or playing a strange game with his fingers.

Every attempt I made to join him in his strange play was rebuffed. He simply wasn't interested in me and was only happy when left alone. I felt like a bystander.

At twelve months of age he attended a child care center for a half-day a week—mainly so I could have a rest. Following a suggestion from staff that he might be hyperactive, I took him to be assessed at the local university special education center. They found his behavior to be "hyperactive" but warned that labeling children with disorders was detrimental.

As the years passed, and with no answers regarding his behavior, I watched as my child remained uninterested in others, hyperactive, and impulsive. Simple outings became disasters—his failure to understand the concept of taking turns and his hyperactivity led to some embarrassing encounters with other parents. Windows, roads, and even clotheslines became potential danger spots as he climbed on, through, or over anything he could.

Depressed and confused and still with no support, I scolded myself for my failure as a parent. Wary of the comments of others, I virtually stopped talking to people and going out in large crowds. It was just easier on me that way.

At age four my son was not properly toilet trained or speaking in sentences. Desperate, I asked if he could join a special education class for some individualized help before going to school, but I was told he did not qualify because of his "short attention span."

I dreaded his going to school. The teacher called me during his first week to discuss his strange behavior and to ask what was wrong with him. At school, I was told, he wandered and daydreamed and was distractible, disorganized, possessive of certain objects, and became easily frustrated and upset. Later I learned he had also endured a great deal of teasing and cruel jokes from other students and that the teachers considered him a naughty nuisance and treated him accordingly.

I requested he receive some individual attention at school but instead was subjected to questions about our home life and discipline habits. I was approached by teachers so frequently with complaints about his behavior that I began to avoid them. I didn't want to hear one more negative thing about him because that's all I ever heard. There were so many wonderful things about my son—I needed to hear some of those.

I didn't want to hear one more negative thing about him because that's all I ever heard.

At times I was torn between frustration at others and their attitude toward my son, and frustration with my son for failing to learn so many basic rules of life.

No matter what I did and who I asked for advice, my son didn't improve. He continued to do unusual things: walking on his toes, being obsessive and fearful of certain objects, showing little of the usual childish interest in Christmas or birthday celebrations. I wanted desperately to take him out of school, but the absence of any diagnosis meant I was effectively trapped in the system with no other way out.

I had been working part-time as a registered nurse in an acute care area, but the responsibility of making critical decisions there, plus the difficulties created by my son, eventually became too much. I opted to quit my job and concentrate solely on my child. At the time I thought I'd made the right decision, but the change meant I no longer had an outlet, a place that took me away from my problems and allowed me to feel normal for a while.

When my son was eight, he was diagnosed with ADHD and started on Ritalin, which helped his concentration greatly. The relentless teasing at school continued, however, and he became so unhappy that he confessed to wanting to die. A counselor advised me than an eight-year-old was unlikely to act on suicidal thoughts—a fact that barely consoled me. The thought of my lovely boy wanting to die because he'd had enough of the world at the age of eight was too much to even think about. He'd cry and say, "Mom, I'm not meant for this world. Please kill me, I'm a freak." He knew he was different, and he hated the world. I felt utterly hopeless.

From time to time over the next few years he would beg me to kill him. He took to walking around the house with a rope around his neck telling me he wished he were an animal because it would be easier that way. He was severely depressed and required psychiatric care and medication. Some nights I'd sit by his bed all night to be sure he didn't try to kill himself.

When my son was twelve years old, he was finally given the diagnosis I had been searching for his entire life. He had Asperger's syndrome, an autistic spectrum disorder. The news was both hugely upsetting and a huge relief. At least a diagnosis would enable him to get the professional help he had needed for so long—or so I thought. I soon discovered that he was now considered too old for any available program or special-needs class. My son had a right to an appropriate education just like any other child, yet now we couldn't get that for him.

For a time we considered moving to the United States or Great Britain, where we had heard of schools and programs suited to his needs. While this idea eventually fell by the wayside, my intense anger remained. After all those years of waiting, of asking questions, of appeasing people and keeping my hopes up, I finally had the answer I had fought so long for. And now it seemed to have all come too late to help him.

He started begging me again to take him out of school and allow him to be home-schooled. This time I agreed, and this has proven to be an absolute joy. I don't know what he actually learned in all his years at school, but I do know he is learning plenty at home every day, thanks to a little common sense and teaching directed at his needs.

I realize now that I removed him from school just in time—before I lost him. It is wonderful to see him learn and discover things in his own way. He's quite a bright boy. I only wish I'd done it from the beginning instead of wasting so much time.

Not Enough Time

SALLY LONG

"TAMMY HAS AGENESIS of the corpus callosum," they said. That meant nothing to us. My husband demanded that the medical talk be dropped, and asked to please put it in English so we could understand. So it was explained. *Agenesis* means "absence," and the corpus callosum is the center section of the brain. It joins the two sides of the brain together and acts like a nerve center, relaying messages and telling our bodies what to do. It tells us when to sit down, to stand, to roll over, everything our bodies do. Our little girl didn't have this part of her brain, therefore she would never progress any farther. She would never walk, talk, feed, or toilet herself and she was given a life span of only twenty years. We were told she would never improve, to expect a downhill run, and basically just to give her the best possible care until she died.

It was devastating: a life span never occurred to me. I always knew it was a major thing we were facing, but this was just beyond belief. To look at my twelve-month-old baby and know that what she was doing now, which was only smiling, crying, and being spoon- and bottle-fed, was all that she would ever do was just beyond belief.

Suddenly our home was overrun with people caring for *our* child. *That was my job!* I felt more like a nurse than a mother. It was all just happening too fast, and there was no time to adjust. Where was the time for the diagnosis to sink in? There wasn't any. We needed time to grieve for the loss of our hopes and dreams for our daughter's life, but we weren't given that. I wanted to scream for everyone to get out of my house.

It sounds terrible, but I dread Tammy's birthdays, not just because it means another year has gone by and they are fast running out, but because I feel guilty if we don't celebrate her birthdays and buy her presents, but it's really just a waste of money. She doesn't know it's her birthday, it's just another day to her. What is the point of wrapping a present for your child when you know she will show no interest in it, and then unwrapping it for her? Why make a birthday cake when she can't blow out the candles, make a wish, or eat a piece of cake? Christmases are just the same. Mother's Day is especially hard. All I hope for is one smile—sometimes I get it, sometimes I don't.

My husband and I have separated a few times over the years; at the moment we are trying again. Our daughter's disability has put a great strain on our relationship. So much time was focused on her that there was none left for us.

I blamed myself for her disability for a long time. Maybe I did something wrong during the pregnancy, or was it because I had stopped breathing during her delivery, but that wasn't true. We went through a period of trying to find out why this had happened. Somehow I thought it would help to have somewhere to lay the blame, somewhere to direct the anger at being robbed of a normal child. There was so much anger and sometimes we directed it at each other.

Sometimes she feels like a burden, as terrible as that sounds. Our boys are now aged thirteen and nine and want to go to the movies, swimming, and so on with mom and dad, but Tammy can't go the movies or swimming, so I let my husband take the boys, and Tammy and I stay home. I watch the three of them walk off, laughing and playing together. It's a mixture of happiness and sadness. When I come back inside, it's nice to have a quiet house, but I feel so lonely and left out. They come home with all their chatter about what they did, how much fun they had, and sometimes it's hard not to be angry with them, but it's not their fault. It's just the way it is, and the boys have missed out on so much already. I guess some of this story sounds bitter and, yes, there is bitterness in me, along with anger, sadness, frustration, and despair. All mixed with such a longing that I don't know how to describe it.

If I've learned anything in the last six years, it's to treasure the little things. With my boys, when they first smiled, I just knew that they would always smile and I knew they would roll over and sit up and crawl and walk and run. Tammy has taught me to never take anything for granted. She has suffered so much more in her six years than I have in my whole life and still she seems so contented, so much at peace. She just seems to accept her life as it is, which is something I think we can all learn from.

I have my good days, when I can look at all the positives—at least I have my daughter. It could have been worse; she could have died at birth or before now. At least she smiles at me, she is such a happy child, and I know she loves me.

Then I have the bad days. So many tears have been shed, often all over Tammy. There is such a deep sadness, a grief because of what is lost and can never be returned. We have been given nothing to hope for, nothing to work toward. Our job is just to give her the best possible care until her life is over, and that's not fair.

Sometimes I am so angry I feel like putting my fists through things and screaming at the injustice of it all. I think the worst feeling is the helplessness, the knowing that there is nothing I can do that will change this. No matter how much I wish Tammy to be normal, no matter how much love and care I give her, it won't change the end result. I'll only have her for about another fourteen years and that's just not enough. Some nights when I tuck my baby into bed, the reality hits that one more day has just gone by. I can't imagine life without her. I wish I had the power to hold back time, but I don't. I know the day will come, and I guess I will deal with it, but it is not something I chose to think about.

Our children can teach us so much more than anyone else ever can. Tammy never doubts that I love her and will always care for her. She doesn't say it in words, but it is there in her little eyes every time we look at each other. She is my inspiration and will always be my little angel.

A Line Drawn in the Sand

DEDE DANKELSON

"THERE'S SOMETHING WRONG with the baby." Those were the words from the maternal-fetal specialist who read my twenty-week ultrasound. His next sentence was equally devastating: "You may want to terminate the pregnancy."

After several years of trying to conceive and being overjoyed at finally achieving a pregnancy, my husband and I knew that under no circumstances would we terminate. That day changed my life forever. It was like a line drawn in the sand—the "before" and the "after" of who I was and who I am struggling to become. It's the day I started on a journey I still travel, and still don't understand.

My son, Peter, was born at thirty weeks weighing two pounds thirteen and a half ounces. He had surgery for a tracheotomy to secure his airway at four days old and spent the first three and a half months of his life in neonatal intensive care. He was diagnosed with Goldenhar syndrome within his first week of life. Peter is fed through a gastrostomy tube, has only one kidney, vertebrae anomalies, a cleft palate, and is missing his left ear.

My son is only eighteen months old, so I have merely scratched the surface of living as this new person. Becoming a mother of any child is a life-changing experience. Becoming a mother of a premature child with multiple congenital anomalies not only changes your life, it requires you to become someone completely new. It forces you to face challenges that seem insurmountable. The emotional aspects alone have left me feeling completely raw. I bear the scars of wounds cut too deeply to put into words.

I am still working through the grief, the "why me," the isolation (despite a loving husband and family) and even the ensuing depression that's all part of the healing process. My emotions and coping abilities have been stretched beyond capacity. My marriage has been both weakened and strengthened. I constantly feel as though I'm undergoing an identity crisis. At this stage in the transformation, I can't even bring myself to remember the "before" me. I have lost nearly all contact with work colleagues and old business associates. I have changed so completely that it is beyond my current capacity to go back in time.

The wounds I carry today remain open, although most people I encounter do not understand the transformation that is occurring within me. My wish is that some day these wounds will become mere scars, a mark to remind me of what I have experienced.

It's true that you must grieve the loss of the child and the experience you anticipated during pregnancy. Unfortunately there is not much time to deal with that grief when you become the parent and caretaker of a special-needs child. I stress the word *caretaker* because that is the role I was least prepared for. All parents are caretakers to some degree, but I believe it's typically more of a supporting role. For me the caretaker role has become my primary job, especially since my son is very fragile medically. Over the past eighteen months I have spent nearly 100 percent of my time in hospitals, at clinic visits, dealing with insurance issues, learning about state and community assistance, educating myself about medical terms and conditions, taking my son to therapy, and chatting via the Internet with other parents. There is nearly no time left for just being a mom. I am getting better at managing all these new responsibilities and I'm hoping that I can continue educating myself in even more areas that affect my son's life.

I am finally starting to change the "mom" versus "caretaker" roles around a bit. Of course the caretaker responsibilities will continue, and they have, in fact, been as demanding as ever. I know also that I will remain in a constant state of worry over medical test results and upcoming surgeries. Those are issues that will never go away completely.

Being a mom, though, is the role I want to spend more time in. I'm trying to make time each day for play and special time with my son. In many ways he has the same needs as any child. He needs love and security, hugs and kisses, playtime and bedtime stories, food and diaper changes, and Band-Aids on his "ouchies." He has already endured more in his short life than I would ever have thought possible. He has the most amazing ability to get through a painful experience and immediately give me a hug. How does he know, I wonder, that I'm not intentionally putting him through all this? How is it that someone so small can know that I, the mom and caretaker, hurt as much from his pain as he does?

I have peered into the depths of my soul more than I ever desired.

I have a college degree, worked as a professional for many years, and traveled around the world a bit. I was thrilled when I became pregnant and, as most women do, envisioned my new life as a mother. That vision, of course, was shattered with those awful words at my twenty-week ultrasound. The new person I am becoming—the "after"—is a person that I cannot begin to envisage. The only thing I'm certain about is that the "after" person will be better. I have peered into the depths of my soul more deeply than I ever desired and am able to endure more than I ever thought possible. I have my son to thank for that.

The Kaleidoscope of Our Life

Faith Sandles

As we watch our daughter come up the brick walk to the front door, I think of what a kaleidoscope our life has been. It is certainly not what we anticipated. We had no specific dreams for our baby when she was born, only that she continue to be healthy and happy.

She charmed everyone who met her, was usually content and very bubbly. The little hints that there might be something wrong were not detected, even by her pediatrician. It was when she was three that a new pediatrician sent us to a neurologist with the news that there was something amiss. The words "she will always have to be supervised but she should be able to drive a car" in the same sentence would be a forewarning of the confusion we were to face over the ensuing years. Although the situation at that early stage sapped my husband and me of our energy, we still feel the same energy drain even today, twenty-four years later.

My husband and I have always been happy together, happy with our daughter, and we have managed to create a very satisfying life, devoting much of our time to ensuring her safety, health, and happiness.

Early on we made an unconventional choice by sending our daughter to a wonderful private facility. Because of the fantastic programs of this school, Abby has had friends from the time she was age three whom she still sees in her day and recreation programs. We have also been very focused on her happiness. My husband has chosen not to play golf each weekend, but to stay home with us instead, and has worked two jobs at times when speech lessons were needed. We have spent most of our volunteer efforts on committees, councils, and boards within the disabilities arena, and we are now both working professionally in the field of disabilities. We feel that this gives us insight into our daughter's needs and personality, but that it also keeps us current with "the system." It has been very rewarding and also keeps us in touch with hundreds of other families with similar challenges.

We have also made the choice not to move to another state, an area we love, so that Abby can stay with the current school. We just want to ensure that she has the very best life possible, especially when we are no longer here. That's the scenario that continues to awaken me at night from a sound sleep.

We would make the same life choices again, given the opportunity, and there are no regrets.

As we approach the final major decision—residential options for our daughter—it is with very mixed feelings. We would like to have her live with us longer, but we want her to become secure in her own home, with a few friends, while we can still oversee her new way of life. This transition will be very difficult for all of us.

There has been grief along the way already and there will be grief again. I'm certain that this grief will continue to be present with us throughout our entire life. I suspect that most families who love and care for a person with developmental disabilities have some form of low-grade depression throughout their lives. It takes many different forms since each family is different, but I truly believe that it is there for all of us. And it is often undetected, not only by the family but also by friends and relatives. I know that our Christian faith has helped us through every stage of this challenge.

My husband and I need to have time together with each other—just to be able to go to a movie instead of planning ahead and hoping for respite that may not be available. We need to be able to go for walks together (she no longer thinks this is fun and refuses to go, and we are unable to leave her alone). We would like to be able to take a short weekend or weeklong trip without the additional fee for a sitter.

However, after twenty-four years, I have come to the belief

that every family, with or without disabilities, has challenges throughout their life. Some disappear, others remain—and they are all different. But we all have the kaleidoscope of colors and pieces! It is how we face this life and how we view the colors and pieces that gives us the quality of life we have.

Acceptance

Life has no other discipline to impose, if we
would but realize it,
than to accept life unquestioningly.

HENRY MILLER

Introduction

Neil Nicoll

Human nature dictates that we will change whatever we can and worry about those things we cannot. The acceptance of unpleasant truths is not something that comes easily to most of us. Yet for parents raising special-needs children, achieving some degree of acceptance is vital to their longer-term prospects for happiness.

What Is Acceptance?

Acceptance is a slippery beast, and difficult to concisely define. In its most basic form, acceptance is said to be achieved when an individual has overcome their feelings of profound grief, shock, anger, and denial over a loss or personal tragedy, and is able to view the event and its effects within the greater context of their entire existence.

All parenting involves some degree of accepting situations and feelings that may not necessarily be all that palatable or in line with personal expectations. For the parents of a child with disabilities, these compromises are significantly magnified.

"Accepting" the birth of a disabled child can be as simple as coming to terms with the reality of your situation and the demands that it imposes upon you. It may involve nothing more than an understanding that there is too much to do to allow yourself ample time to grieve. While useful as a short-term coping mechanism, the deferral of grieving is not an emotionally healthy option in the longer term. Emotional conflicts left unaddressed do not simply vanish but remain "buried" within the psyche and can have a negative impact at a later date.

Learning to Let Go

The process of moving toward acceptance in its truest form involves the letting go of emotional connections to the past, letting go of hopes and expectations, and acknowledging things as they truly are, not how you wish they could be.

Acceptance is often the end of the process of telling your story. For families with a disabled child this process can involve considerable pain and angst, but it can also be a liberating and even joyful experience. Acceptance has its own rewards. It often brings with it the freedom to live life largely free of past emotional burdens, to place things into a different perspective. Accepting your child's disability doesn't imply that you are content with your life, or that your child's condition no longer causes you any anguish. Instead, it implies that you acknowledge the difficulties of your situation but can also see the many other positives that exist in your life and have the strength and willingness to actively seek them out.

Acceptance is often the end of the process of telling your story.

From my work with parents I have found that the period of acceptance is marked by a revival of old interests and pursuits that had previously been abandoned or pushed into the background. From simple pleasures, such as celebrating their child's small achievements, to more systemic life challenges such as career, relationships, and other responsibilities, life begins to take on a more balanced and complete feel. The past is never forgotten, but instead of being a constant burden, it becomes a lesson from which parents draw hope, inspiration, and confidence.

It's no surprise that many parents feel they are quite significantly changed by the process of accepting their child's disability. Many speak of finding a greater strength of character and purpose, of feeling proud that they have survived one of life's toughest challenges. They may feel renewed strength and determination to care for their child and may even decide to take on some additional challenges.

The period of acceptance is also a stage when many parents feel they have a great deal to offer others in similar circumstances. This may involve everything from taking a more active leadership role in support groups, volunteering to help at their child's school, or simply listening to others and offering heartfelt advice. The many parent stories in this book all reveal some degree of acceptance, and all reflect the honesty and pride that stem from the long journey these people have traveled.

The Closure Myth

The term *closure* has become something of a psychological buzzword in recent years. It's a mantra reinforced by every TV psychologist and best-selling self-help author—your problem cannot be solved, your pain cannot be considered over, until you have reached "closure."

If only human beings were so straightforward. But they are not. The very term *closure* implies an ending, a sense of finality. Acceptance for the parents of special-needs children cannot ever be really final or complete, not only because the source of their sadness—the child—remains as a reminder of their pain, but also because human beings can seldom resist asking themselves "what if?"

"I know my child will never talk, but what if he could say a few words one day?"

"Wouldn't it be great if my daughter could make that mainstream class one day? The teachers say she just can't do it, but you never know."

"Wouldn't it be great if he could just join in a soccer game with the other children?"

There is absolutely nothing wrong with such musings, in fact they are completely understandable. These people are not in denial, they are merely being human. One parent I met had taken these thoughts to another level. She imagined a "wouldn't it be nice" box into which she mentally assigned the hopes and dreams for her child that were beyond her reach, possibly forever.

This may not be the much vaunted "closure," but it certainly is a positive form of acceptance. The ability to objectify your emotional reactions, to stand apart from them, to observe them, to live a full life despite your regrets, and to embrace your child for what he or she is, is proof positive of a healthy personality.

Dance Recitals Are Still Possible

Becky Whidden Huff

"I HATE TO RUIN YOUR DAY, but . . ."

Little did I know the impact those few words would have on my life. Less than twelve hours after the birth of my daughter, Lily, my doctor used those words and with them, delivered the blow of a lifetime.

As the words "Down syndrome" spilled awkwardly from his lips, postpartum elation turned to shock. I looked at my husband, Parks, and he stared back in disbelief. As my doctor continued talking, I began to feel angry. How could he come into my room on one of the happiest days of my life and say such a thing? Lily was my baby, my perfect little miracle. Why couldn't he just let us be? And yet somewhere in the depths of my soul, I knew it was true.

I refused sleeping pills that first night, scared that I would wake feeling relieved it was all just a terrible dream, only to live it all over again. I had been so pleased that an epidural had taken away the pain of childbirth. Now I wished for something to dull my feelings of pain and sorrow instead. Emotions were high as we began spreading the news to family and friends. I began taking on their pain as well as my own, feeling somehow responsible.

My pain only deepened when I learned the day after her birth that Lily would need heart surgery in the coming months to close two holes and repair a valve. From that moment on, I was in an emotional holding pattern until she came through surgery.

The cardiologist who delivered the news of her heart condition told us the surgery couldn't be performed until Lily was strong enough to handle it. This meant it was vital that she gain an appropriate amount of weight. I made a decision that very night not to nurse her, even though I was already using a breast pump to encourage my milk along. It would be impossible to accurately gauge how much milk Lily was receiving if I breast-fed, and I simply couldn't bear any additional stress. My engorged breasts over the next few days added to my sorrow and I cried more than I have ever done in my life.

For a long time I mourned the Lily I had dreamed of: the beautiful, bright little girl who would charm us in her dance recitals and make us cry at her wedding. Close friends and family would ask if it would have been easier if I'd known about the Down syndrome before her birth. I responded by telling them I believed God disguised it to protect me from adding undue stress to my pregnancy. In any case, I was jolted into acceptance by the need to nurture and love my baby above all else.

At nearly five months of age, Lily came through open-heart surgery with flying colors. We soon resumed her physical therapy, which had been cut back because it was burning too many of the precious calories she needed to grow. The simple act of eating used to leave her feeling exhausted. The nurses told us the surgery would breathe new life into Lily. We saw that materialize as she began eating with vigor, becoming more animated and alert with each day that passed.

Lily is now seven months old, and I don't pretend to know all the challenges that lie ahead. But I can say that I let go of my imagined Lily and truly embraced the wonderful child God has placed in my care.

I'm learning that we can't set limitations on our children. I want her to reach her full potential. I have the same hopes for Lily as I have for her brother. Dance recitals are still possible, if she chooses. Her weekly physical and speech therapy sessions coupled with daily "homework" are helping her develop by leaps and bounds.

Down syndrome is a part of who Lily is, but it certainly doesn't define her as a person. Those who love her will make sure of that.

Just the other day, I caught a glimpse of Lily as I was passing by a mirror. I saw her perhaps as a stranger would, Down syndrome and all. Yet when I look at her, I see her the way God must see her—through eyes that reflect unconditional love and acceptance.

Sure, my life has changed with Lily's diagnosis. My heart has opened in ways I could never have imagined and I've seen the very best in others as they have reached out and embraced my family. I'm learning to take each day as it comes and stop fretting over the small stuff.

I know there are many difficult times ahead, but Lily is helping me face each day with humor, grace, hope, and love.

I Believe in Miracles

Dawn Proudlove

I WAS INTRODUCED to my daughter this spring, April 2nd, to be precise. That was also the day I learned I had underestimated my child's potential and failed to recognize her true strength.

We stood together in front of sixty-five students and three teachers at our local Christian school. I had been invited to speak about disability issues to students grades five and six. The school had been delighted when I informed them that my fifteen-year-old daughter, Jenna, who was confined to a wheelchair with cerebral palsy, would be available to join me.

As any good mother will do in an attempt to ensure that her child doesn't fail in an endeavor, I took time before the school presentation to prepare Jenna for her "part." I had a litany of information I fed her on a daily basis, including such wisdom as "Remember, the kids are there to learn about disabilities, so we don't want to be negative and talk about all those that have ignored you and hurt you" and "Remember, don't get into a laughing fit. We need to be professional." Then of course, we had to review the agenda I had prepared while prompting Jenna on her "lines." We were still reviewing that agenda one last time as we pulled into the school parking lot.

I was nervous. I had spoken to many groups on many issues, but had never presented with my daughter before. I began to doubt the wisdom of my decision and made a mental note to control the agenda so that Jenna didn't feel stressed and uncomfortable. Sixty-five faces looked expectantly at us as I introduced Jenna and myself. Then, with more than a little trepidation, I turned the floor over to Jenna so that she could tell her peers a little about herself.

And that is when the miracle happened! That is when I was given the miracle of meeting the person who is my child.

"A grandchild is a miracle, but a renewed relationship with your own children is even a greater one." (T. Berry Brazelton, pediatrician and author)

Such a moment of clarity! For the next two hours I watched my daughter move through each item on the agenda with confidence and intuitiveness. I watched her share her personal experiences, her joys and sorrows, with sensitivity and honesty. I watched this young woman encourage timid and fearful youths into asking the most personal questions and then answer, with a wisdom that could only have been God given. I was enthralled! And I was humbled.

The realization came to me that I had been paying lip service when I extolled my daughter's abilities in the past. I knew then that I had only been celebrating her strengths within the context of her "disabilities." When others had remarked on Jenna's abilities, I had attached disclaimers. As proud of her as I was, I had failed to "see" my daughter through the same eyes I used to view my other, non-disabled children. I had filtered Jenna's gifts and achievements, as well as her failures, through the lens of disability.

That day I was presented with a miracle that few parents are fortunate enough to ever experience. The miracle of seeing my daughter in all her strengths and weaknesses.

Since that day I have been reflecting on many things: on Jenna's right to choose her own path in life, on my hope for a system that will accommodate her dream, on the wealth of possibilities that her future holds. I believe in miracles!

And in my heady, giddy anticipation I recall the words of Pablo Picasso: "Everything is a miracle. It is a miracle that one does not dissolve in one's bath like a lump of sugar."

Making the Right Choices

DON WARD

IT TOOK ME TOO LONG to realize that the best days are when I unclog the toilet. For a long time I chose to believe those were the bad days. I was wrong.

It may be an accident that my autistic son, Doug, has colitis. The colitis may also be the result of taking a certain drug to suppress seizures. An entry-level health care professional believed that Doug was experiencing cluster seizures when he drifted into inattention. CAT scans and electroencephalograms never found any evidence of seizures. So, after several years on seizure medication, Doug's neurologist discontinued the treatment. I just learned that certain drugs can eat away at the stomach lining and cause colitis. Other medications that may help relieve anxiety aggravate the colitis. Colitis is painful. The pain causes aggression, which requires medication that causes aggression. And so on and on.

In the early days I chose to pursue the neurological cure for autism. I also pursued the behavioral cure, the nutritional cure, the metaphysical and spiritual cure, the situation-management cure, the environmental cure, and the when-things-get-tough-let's-go-for-a-ride-to-see-the-power-lines cure.

Now, in the days that precede my plumbing exercise, Doug's eyes become glassy, his echolalia escalates, and his tone becomes guttural. He withdraws to his inner world where he gets "pay-per-view" in his head, like his own private TV show. He's irritable and lashes out, mostly when he's at school. If I could, I would choose plumbing over first aid every time.

When choosing medications, I can make bad choices. There

are those that sedate Doug. They make him agreeable, or at least submissive. They also make him unresponsive, remote, and cold. There have been times when I chose medications that let him be himself. I would choose to hear him laugh, even if an insane cackle was the result.

My little boy's first sentence was "I bite," at about thirteen months. It was a few months before he spoke another complete sentence that predicted Doug would later show violent tendencies and that he would master expressive as well as receptive communications. Early on, I chose to emphasize his intellectual gifts and play down his aggression. It didn't matter that I wanted to showcase his talents—he won't cooperate when he's observed or tested. He does this to torment me. Sometimes he even bites the test administrator.

I've caught Doug showing some unexpected and hidden skills. Until he was nine, he was able to mentally group fairly large numbers of objects and instantly report the total. He let me know that he could do this with as many as twenty-six objects. I don't know if that was his limit, or if he has a limit, or if he can count cards.

He also surprised me two years ago by revealing that he could accurately write the names of the characters from *Toy Story*, the name Toys "R" Us, and a number of fast-food-related words and phrases. He dealt with these as a gestalt, or a pattern, rather than a series of letters. In my competitive zeal for educational performance, I insisted on math and writing rigor in school and at home. Doug was taught "bubble numbers," where, for example, the number two is decorated with two bubbles. He can't successfully count more than three bubbles without error. He has lost interest in learning new words. I made a choice to show the world that Doug's "moderately retarded" label was wrong. I chose to stretch Doug's intellectual capacity and it snapped.

A number of years ago, at the height of the Christmas rush, we stood in the toy store breadline, many parents and wailing children deep. Doug's echolalia sprang forth. "Take your hands off me! I'll call the police!" he shrieked in imitation of movie dialogue. At once the toy-store pandemonium went silent. Every head turned to me. I turned my palms upward and chose to be embarrassed.

I made a series of choices to raise Doug as a single dad. Two years ago I decided to extend that to a full-time position. I'm demanding, impatient, exacting, picky, self-centered, silent. Doug has chosen to ignore these qualities altogether and he has made me better for it.

I have a friend who is smart. She is as smart as any unafflicted person can be. She accuses me of enjoying the pain of martyrdom. She knows that I revere Don Quixote, Saint Lawrence, Mucius Scaevola, and all the other martyrs of history and literature. The difference, of course, is that hero-martyrs did not make choices. They accepted the truth and lived with the consequences, no matter how dire. My path was different. I tried to impose my will on autism. I failed miserably. I made bad choices.

I tried to impose my will on autism. I failed miserably. I made bad choices.

Pinocchio was Doug's favorite movie for a time. As we stood in a food store checkout line, he looked up at me and announced, "Look Father, I'm a real boy now!" I laughed. He ignored me. Sometimes, these days, I make better choices.

Four Boys, No Waiting

SANDRA MILLER

Not a day, hour, minute goes by without someone not listening to me or asking why. Limits are pushed, and my patience is pressed, especially when it's time to get dressed. Nothing gets done without one-on-one supervision—slow them down to speed them up, with all this hurry we can't catch up!

I knew kids would be hard, but being physically and emotionally trapped daily never came to mind. When my eight-month-old crawled up the couch and scaled the cabinets on the wall, I started putting things away. Anticipating hazards most people would not dream of, my pediatrician made sure I knew CPR. After giving birth to the twins I went to the doctor for my two-year-old's checkup. He behaved so appallingly that the doctor told me he would put him on medication when it became necessary.

The twins got meningitis and multiple ear infections. Language and behavior problems soon followed. They were given early intervention and were in school by three years old. Their behavior didn't improve. The schools were saying ADHD, but compared to their older brother I said knew there was no way this could be true.

My oldest never stopped, but he was manageable if he was supervised one-on-one. Engaging, bright, and charming, bubbling all the time except when overstimulated, which happened most often when he was with the twins. The twins were quick but clumsy.

They were often in their own world, detached, appearing not to listen. Poison Control was programmed onto my speed dial after I found one twin flushing towels down the toilet while the other took Dimetapp capsules. He didn't need his stomach pumped, but he slept from one P.M. to nine A.M. the next morning. Anticipating problems with drowning in the toilet, I bought locks. They lasted thirty seconds. My oldest saw the locks and said "that's a bad thing" and broke them off. Toilet patrol occurred regularly after that! I've had to replace a door, a window, two bathroom floors and a tub. It is amazing what a four-year-old can do with a hammer.

With full-time school came evaluations, medications, psychiatrists, psychologists, and sociologists. I sometimes felt like a lousy parent. No matter how many times I show the boys how to organize their things, it is still like having a three-year-old. I'm a broken record day after day—"Clean your room, clothes away!"—walking them through the steps daily. Things most kids can do independently by seven, like put their dirty plates in the sink and clothes in the hamper, they still can't do at ages ten and twelve. On the other hand, I now have a three-year-old who puts his toys away, dishes in the sink, and clothes in the hamper with very little prompting. I feel like God sent me him to let me know I'm not a lousy parent.

I quickly learned not to trust social workers. I don't think they have enough psychological background to deal with my boys. As much as the boys don't listen, they have radar to give people what they want if it will cause a problem. All it takes is a few leading questions. The funny thing is I don't think they do it on purpose. The twins do this more than my oldest. My oldest will outright threaten me with calling the police or the Department of Youth Services to attempt to get his way. I look forward to the summer medication break so I won't have to deal with the Dr. Jekyll and Mr. Hyde effect that the medications give them.

Dealing with naturally wired kids is easier for me than is the nightly withdrawal from the stimulant medications. Even though they are forgetful, there is a lot less tension in the house. The psychiatrists say that the boys need to have the drugs all year so that they can develop and remain in control. I think they socialize better without the drugs because of the withdrawal factor.

The twins both do things to alienate their peers, overreacting to things they don't like, ignoring people who are trying to be friendly, and trying to force themselves into games others are playing. They are very smart and test high in math and language, but they are socially inept.

I can't begin to express the frustration and embarrassment of having to stand beside them wherever we are because I know that, even with me next to them, a problem will occur. You just have to be there to stop it from getting worse when it happens. The moments of normal behavior do happen, but I have a totally different concept of what good behavior is than other people do. I still get looks and attitudes even when they aren't being that bad. Maybe that's because I have to praise the twins a lot about the good things when they do happen, and because I have to redirect them so many times when they're being "bad."

After a bad day out with the kids I sometimes wish I were single again. I feel like running away or giving them away. I think anyone who sees my kids may not want to have any of their own, and I can see why some people may consider adoption. I then have to remember all the good things they have done. I think about the smiles, like when the twins used sign language to describe a moose they had seen. I think about the poems they have written, the silly jokes they tell, the compliments they have received for the suits they like to wear while all the other kids are wearing Goth or baggy clothes.

I think about the psychologist who told me he had never seen a child with such high moral values as my oldest child. I think about the times he sticks up for his brothers, even though he can't stand them. And the interest they all show in things I would never have given a second thought to.

The world would not be the same without them.

Blessed

DONNA TACK

Where to begin? At the beginning, I guess.

On August 15, 2001, I gave birth to a beautiful, healthy baby boy. I don't think I've ever experienced that kind of happiness before in my life. Spencer was so beautiful and perfect. Oh, the plans I had for him—for us. They were boundless. He would love books, I dreamed, be great at sports, maybe become a scientist, architect, or doctor. The list went on.

On September 22, 2001, all those dreams suddenly came crashing down around me.

Spencer was born with a problem called gastroesophageal reflux disease. "Nothing to worry about," they told me. "Very common," they told me. Yet early that fateful morning, while in the care of a nurse, my beautiful boy had a reflux episode and stopped breathing. The nurse whom I entrusted with my precious son was not watching him; the monitor the doctor had ordered for Spencer was not on. He was left not breathing for so long that his poor little heart finally just stopped beating. That is how they found him.

The fact that they were able to get his heart going again is, to me, a miracle in itself. It all seems so surreal now, looking back: the frantic hours spent in the intensive care unit of the hospital, the endless disbelief that this nightmare was really happening. "It's not real," I told myself over and over . . . and over. But, pray as I might, it was real.

Spencer looked so small in the heated crib they had him in, and there were so many tubes and wires and machines that I could barely get close to him. The room was dark but for the light of all those machines, and I swear to you, it didn't seem real. I was simply having a very vivid nightmare and I would wake up. But, of course, I didn't.

When our son was barely five weeks old, we were told he had been "severely, catastrophically, globally brain damaged." I think I crumbled then. I'm not sure, it was all a blur. I didn't think it was possible to feel that kind of pain and still live. I'm here to tell you it is.

I didn't think it was possible to feel that kind of pain and still live. I'm here to tell you it is.

Over the next few weeks we saw every "ology" in the hospital. Cardiology, endocrinology, neurology, and on and on. Spencer needed surgery to get a feeding tube inserted since he had lost the ability to suck and swallow on his own. The surgery did not go well, and afterward we were told there was nothing more that could be done for him. Our son was given only days to live.

I spent that long night holding my son in my arms and cursing every god that ever was. I cried tears I didn't even know I had left. How could life be so viciously cruel? I was so empty and bitter inside, I thought I would die.

Arrangements were quickly made for Spencer to be transferred to a palliative care hospice for his final days. My husband and I had gone to the hospice with heavy hearts, resigned to saying good-bye to the son we had never been given a chance to know. The hospice was a beautiful, renovated old mansion. A very warm and spiritual place. I felt at peace the moment we crossed the threshold. Spencer was given a crib in front of a big, beautiful window. My husband and I were both allowed to stay with him, something we hadn't been able to do for weeks. We were a family again.

Within days of arriving, Spencer started to stabilize. Another miracle! After three weeks we were moved to yet another place— a rehab center.

After a month spent being "trained" to meet our son's very specialized needs, we were all able to go home. What a scary day that was! I couldn't believe that I was now going to be solely responsible for this child who required suctions and oxygen, feeding machines and a list of medications that made my head swim. But home we went.

Now, many months later, how do I feel? Blessed! Spencer is still with us. We have been in and out of hospital several times for any number of problems. I still get scared. I still feel sorry for myself. I still feel angry and bitter and cheated. I still ask why.

But do you know what? I feel those things so much less. I love my son as much as, if not more than, I ever thought it was possible to love another human being. I have become a nurse, a doctor, a physiotherapist, an occupational therapist, and so many other specialties I couldn't even begin to tell you.

I laugh again. I trust again. I feel again. I wouldn't have thought it possible not so long ago. I can't imagine my life without Spencer. Do I ever wish that this had never happened, that Spencer was "normal"? Every day! But I can't change what was, I can only make the very best of what is.

I know most people wouldn't think so, but I am a very lucky person. I have a husband I love and who loves and supports me, a wonderful close family, and a very special boy named Spencer.

A Baby No Different, So Different

Shona Parekh

It was my first pregnancy. I was thrilled, but at the same time apprehensive of the massive changes that were about to take place. Were Mayank and I ready for parenthood?

My gynecologist took great care of both the developing baby and me. At a routine scan during the fifth month I distinctly remember her saying there were no folds on the back of the baby's neck, and thus no indication of Down syndrome. I remember feeling taken aback, as abnormality had not crossed my mind. And then relief! My perfect life was pretty much on course.

The pregnancy proceeded without a hitch. I remember wishing for our son to inherit my father's good looks. I did not have to pray for a normal, healthy child. That was a given!

The eighth month of the pregnancy was odd.

We had done up the baby's nursery in a clown's theme and caught a documentary on TV of kids with Down syndrome, coincidentally, being entertained by clowns. My heart sank.

Mom got a huge poster for the nursery. It was of a child looking disappointed that his ice-cream scoop had fallen off the cone, with the heading "Why Me?" Again, for some reason, "Why me?" hit me like a powerful punch.

On another occasion, as I waited for the elevator at work, an intellectually challenged girl came up to me and said, "Can I be your friend?" I had no idea where she came from and, taken aback, looked at her and said, "No, I'm sorry, I can't be your friend." The elevator doors opened and I went in alone. As soon as the doors closed, I regretted saying that, and felt as if I had failed a test. As if I had said "No!" to an angel. I went back down, but she was gone.

Zubin decided to make his appearance three weeks earlier than expected, with a textbook-perfect delivery. We were told we had a perfectly normal baby boy—just a little tinier than the doctors expected. When he was placed on me to suckle and hold, I caught a glimpse of a Down syndrome–type expression, but it disappeared after a few seconds. I thought it was my imagination and decided not to say anything to my doctor. And the euphoria of the birth quickly took over.

Later that morning Zubin's pediatrician did his first checks and promptly and confidently announced that we had a perfectly normal healthy baby. The nurses, especially, doted over how cute he was and warned us that girls would be throwing themselves at him!

Zubin was discharged as scheduled, and we went home in a jubilant mood. It was only when he was readmitted to the hospital's neonatal unit after four days with severe jaundice that I voiced my concerns to Mayank about Zubin's "Down syndrome." He reminded me that many doctors had looked at him but had said nothing.

The very next day our pediatrician summoned us to his clinic for a "discussion." We listened with a heavy heart as he explained, as sensitively as he could, his suspicions. He said he had noticed several physical features that pointed to Down syndrome, but that he could not be sure. He said that the diagnosis could only be confirmed by a blood test, which we agreed to. He asked if anyone had commented that Zubin was "funny-looking"?

Some thoughts that crossed my mind included the fear that Mayank would blame me, or might even want a divorce. But for both of us, the immediate reactions was to do our best for Zubin. That same afternoon Mayank went to the library to get books on Down syndrome. That reassured me that Mayank was there for both of us.

Walking back to Zubin's crib in the neonatal unit felt surreal, as if I was walking in slow motion. There was a distinct absence of nurses around him, as if he had some kind of deadly, contagious disease. Hurting as we did, we put up our bravest front. We carried our clueless, innocent child, gathered his things, and confronted the world with heads held high. I felt so much more protective about Zubin.

We carried our clueless, innocent child, gathered his things, and confronted the world with heads held high.

Earlier, we had sent out cards to friends all over the world announcing Zubin's birth. I wondered if we had to send them another card explaining Zubin's condition. We decided that we did not want to put any label on Zubin and would treat him as "normally" as we could. Apart from my parents, we did not confide in anyone. They said Zubin was lucky to have us as parents, and they told us to give him lots of love and milk!

And so the agonizing two-month wait for the result began. While we waited, we swung from positive moments to moments of despair. We did see several other pediatricians, hoping that at least someone would affirm that Zubin was normal.

It was especially hard on me. Mayank would go to work and I would be left at home alone with Zubin. The suspense of waiting for the result was unbearable. Some days I practiced simple exercises with him that I had learned from the library books. Other times I felt this was some form of retribution. Almost every hour, I bargained hard with God.

One day, while giving Zubin his bath, which he enjoyed tremendously, I suddenly wondered if I should let go and let him slip from my fingers. I froze for what seemed like an eternity. I thought I could say that the phone had rung and I left him on his own. But as I stared at Zubin, I wondered how I could have such cold-blooded thoughts about the child in front of me, the child I had not yet even gotten to know.

Two and a half months crawled by. With heart pounding I called the pediatrician. He said the results had just come in, confirming the extra chromosome.

During a postnatal checkup with my gynecologist, she suggested that we change to a pediatrician who was familiar with Down syndrome. And so we did.

The decision to have children after Zubin was difficult on many fronts. Do we focus all our efforts on Zubin and give 100 percent to him? Or would siblings provide him with companionship and be role models? What would we have done under normal circumstances?

When Zubin was nine months old, I got pregnant with our second child. It was happy news but at the same time terrifying. I could not help breaking down and crying.

Our switch of pediatricians must have upset our original pediatrician because eighteen months later, just after the birth of our second child, when we wanted Zubin's original chromosomal test report, he asked in an extra-loud, clear voice, "So, is this one normal?" The short conversation had taken place when Mayank bumped into him along the corridor of the delivery ward. I could hear his insensitive question from inside my room even though the door was closed. It hurt. It was like being stabbed straight in the heart. I felt embarrassed and angry. Incidentally, we never got to keep the original report (despite paying over a hundred dollars), as he wanted it for his records.

During those painful months I had unconsciously stopped enjoying Zubin, his being "baby" and me being "mommy." Once I realized this, I began showering him with mountains of love and formula (the breast-feeding did not work out).

Looking back, I am ceaselessly grateful we did not know we were expecting a child with Down syndrome. With my mind-set at the time and with the kind of lifestyle we led, I know we would have opted for an abortion.

Today, eight years later, I cannot imagine life without Zubin. He has taught me so many lessons, and has so much love in him. He is the one most sensitive to my feelings. One time, after I had punished him in anger and then regretted it and said I was sorry, he unhesitatingly said, "It's okay, Mom," giving me a bear hug and several kisses. I am truly not worthy of such a loving child.

This bit of wisdom off the Internet is a timely reminder to all of us: "I asked God to make my handicapped child whole. God said, 'No. His spirit is whole, his body is only temporary.'"

Empowerment

What lies behind us and what lies before
   us are tiny matters,
Compared to what lies within us.

RALPH WALDO EMERSON

Introduction

NEIL NICOLL

IMAGINE SITTING ON A PLANE, flying thirty thousand feet in the air, when the captain makes the type of announcement that every airline passenger secretly dreads: "Ladies and gentlemen, we are experiencing a mechanical problem with the aircraft. Please remain calm and fasten your seatbelts. . . ."

Those who have listened as a doctor explains that their beloved child has a significant disability can relate to our hapless passenger. Both passenger and parent alike find themselves on a journey that isn't turning out the way anyone expected. Both are frightened. Both are fearful of what comes next. And significantly, faced with a situation over which they have little control, both feel utterly helpless, utterly powerless.

The difference between the two examples is, of course, that while the plane passenger can hope that the pilot saves the day, the parent of a disabled child has only themselves and their loved ones to turn to. Surviving the journey with a special-needs child requires more than a strong seatbelt—it also requires the sort of willpower and inner strength rarely found in those who feel powerless in the hands of life. Empowering yourself and regaining some control over circumstances is an important step in dealing with your child's disability.

Definition

Open a dictionary and you'll see that the word *empower* has three definitions: "to authorize," "to give power to," and "to make able." Let's look at these different nuances in the context of caring for a child with a disability.

"To authorize": Do you recall the scene from the Monty Python movie *The Meaning of Life* in which a doctor cheerfully tells a heavily pregnant woman that she is unable to assist in the birth of her own child because she is "not qualified"? Many parents I meet know exactly how she feels.

Doctors are trained to diagnose, not explain. What makes perfect sense to them often sounds like gobbledygook to those without a medical diploma. Parents often find themselves in a situation where they receive a diagnosis for their child, rapidly followed by a blitzkrieg of technical medical terminology and incomprehensible test results, all issued in a rapid mumble by a specialist they have met only once or twice before.

In this less-than-ideal environment, is it any wonder that questions go unanswered, concerns go unaddressed? Even after the initial shock of diagnosis has passed, parents regularly complain that they feel excluded from the process of making the early, and often very crucial, decisions about their child's treatment. Some go so far as to say that their wishes and ideas were unwelcome, or dismissed as irrelevant. It seems that "doctor knows best" is not as passé a term as one might hope.

So how do average parents extricate themselves from beneath the avalanche of medical jargon? How do they get their opinions to count, their wishes considered? How do they begin to feel "authorized" to make decisions?

They prepare for their appointments with doctors and other specialists beforehand. Make a list of your concerns and questions in advance and take this into the appointment with you. If your child is likely to be disruptive during the appointment, bring someone along to "baby-sit" when you need to speak with the doctor in detail. Some parents initially bring along a professional advocate, friend, or colleague who can assist and support them while they gain confidence. Don't be frightened to stand your ground and insist on your questions being answered. After all, it's your child and it's your money.

Parents need to become mini-medical specialists on their child's particular disability. The Internet is a tremendous research tool, as are public libraries, informational presentations, and lectures. I have attended meetings where the well-prepared and well-read parents are far more knowledgeable about their child's disability than the experts who are there to advise them. Knowledge is power.

Learn to deal with the machinations of bureaucracy. Schools, disability support services, large hospitals, and welfare agencies are all bureaucracies of one kind or another. There is often a mangle of red tape preventing your family from accessing the kind of assistance your child may need. To overcome that hurdle takes diplomacy, grace under pressure, advocacy, and a dose of political savvy. Hone your letter-writing skills and telephone manner; get to know your school principal and your local politicians.

"To give power to": In a political sense, the parents of disabled children are not, and never will be, a powerful force. In any country, the disabled population is generally never more than 10 percent of the total. Further, the "disabled" population does not cluster into any specific geographic area, nor do they act, think, or vote in a cohesive bloc.

Instead, the power of the disabled and their supporters lies in the power of the individual to bring forth improved circumstances for themselves and others in their position. Parents regularly form lobby groups and support organizations through which they can negotiate with government and service providers in a more formal sense. Although they may never sway elections or bring about a change in the public psyche, such groups can be highly regarded and influential in the sense that they can present issues to those in charge and thus become part of the decision-making process.

People take up the "political" banner on behalf of their children for many reasons. For most it is because they truly want to see meaningful change in the quality and amount of services available to children with disabilities. For some, involvement in peak organizations is a means by which they can vent pent-up emotional energy in a constructive manner. For others, getting involved allows them some small degree of control over the grief and loss they feel and offers them distance from the wave of emotion they fear might otherwise engulf them.

You don't have to be chairman of the board to empower yourself. By linking with like-minded families, many discover the opportunity to share experiences, triumphs, and losses and to seek solutions to common problems. Support groups remind families that they are not alone and that others share their experiences and fears. The importance of this realization cannot be overstated; it can be the source of considerable strength and growth for families.

"To make able": As the parent of a disabled child, you will do extraordinary things. Yes, it is true that all parents learn new skills and become adept at managing a range of challenges, but special kids require special abilities. You do not have to become a super parent, but you will become a parent with uncommon skills. Your challenges will be physical, emotional, financial, logistical, intellectual, and above all constant.

> *As the parent of a disabled child, you will do extraordinary things.*

The parents of children with disabilities can do all of the following and more:

- Lift impossible weights safely
- Resolve extraordinary temper tantrums
- Operate sophisticated equipment
- Create special diets
- Administer medications
- Apply the theories and practices from a variety of specialist professions including teaching, speech pathology, occupational therapy, physiotherapy, medicine, social work, and psychology
- Negotiate with difficult and often reluctant bureaucracies
- Deal with periods of prolonged and extraordinary emotional and physical stress
- Lend exceptional support to others
- Balance family and career with all of the above.

Of course, not everyone is equally adept at keeping all these balls in the air at once, which is hardly surprising, given that this is a balancing act of the highest order. For some families, mere survival is a triumph. For these people, empowerment may simply be the ability to cope with today a little better than yesterday.

There are times when empowerment comes from surrender rather than victory. For some parents, a time will come when they realize that caring for their child has simply become impossible and that they need someone else to take over the reins. Being able to let go at certain transition points in the life of a child is a vital part of the parenting role. Letting go sometimes involves a degree of giving up. To face and accept that fact requires an enormous degree of empowerment and raw courage.

Evolution of a Soul

Rebecca Riggs

I LOOK BACK OVER the past twenty-three years and I feel as though I've lived enough for three people.

Over that time my spirit, the very essence of who I am, has changed and grown in ways I once could never have imagined. I was taught early in my life to have no dreams. If you don't have dreams, they cannot be stolen. My son, Erik, not only taught me how to dream again, he helped me to realize that life's possibilities are indeed endless.

I gave birth to Erik over two decades ago, at the age of nineteen. I'd survived a harsh childhood, drifted into marriage, and up until Erik's arrival, I had happily let life drag me where it may.

My son was born with severe cerebral palsy, and we knew right away he would be totally dependent on full-time care for the rest of his life. Suddenly the aimless teenager had an enormous responsibility to face. I began to educate myself about his disability and, little by little, learned to advocate for the services he needed and to become involved in all aspects of his therapy. Before long I began working at the center Erik attended and became increasingly intent on understanding all I could about cerebral palsy and its treatment. Knowledge is indeed a potent drug.

As I empowered myself with learning, the frightened little girl within me began to stand a little taller and a little straighter. Gradually I grew, and for the first time in a long time I began to breathe.

Unfortunately, as I evolved and grew stronger, my husband and I began to grow apart. I was no longer the young girl he had married. I saw life differently than before. I had seen how knowledge and persistence could change people's lives. The new spirit within me was flexing her newly formed muscles, and I became restless and questioning. My marriage eventually ended after the birth of my second son, Jeremy, who will soon turn twenty-one.

Suddenly I was a single mother of a three- and a five-year-old and I tasted what it was like to be my own person for the first time ever. It was an exhilarating, if not sometimes daunting, period. My children and I would load up my little Dodge Colt and drive to the zoo or to see relatives. We never thought about disabilities—we were too busy getting drunk on life and the array of sights and experiences it offered.

Of course, raising Erik was a sometimes difficult task, but with him beside me, I found courage and determination from deep within. I faced doctors, I argued with specialists, I became an expert on my son's condition. When Erik turned sixteen, we were told that, in our home state of Arkansas, the only long-term care option for people like Erik was a nursing home or institution. I had always assumed that Erik would one day live in his own home with outside assistance. To be told that he was not allowed this basic human right, that his only option was to be segregated from society in a huge institution, that he and others like him were not allowed to breathe the air of freedom that most of us take for granted, shocked me to my very core.

I decided to fight back and began advocating even more furiously for my son's rights to everyone who would listen. Erik meanwhile became increasingly despondent over the threat of forced institutionalization. He developed a swallowing disorder in which he aspirated 10 percent of every swallow of liquid he took. As a result, everything had to be thickened to pudding consistency to avoid aspiration. For Erik, this was the final straw. He decided that if he could no longer drink, he would no longer eat either. Erik, so full of life for so long, now wanted to die. For six months, at the same time that I was fighting bureaucracies I also fought with my son, force-feeding him four times a day. The strain became unbearable—I was working full-time, spending hours advocating against his placement in an institution, and watching the light dwindle from my son's eyes at the same time. Finally I had no choice but to have a feeding tube inserted into him. He still has it and has never regained his desire to eat.

As I continued to lobby for changes to the system, news of the plight of Erik and our family reached others. I began to be invited to speak at conferences and was given access to legislators. Not long after I met my second husband, we learned that our fight was finally over—Erik would be allowed to live in his own home with support services. He could live as he wished, where he wished, and with dignity.

For the first time in years, I felt the weight on my shoulders slip away. The iron band of fear that had surrounded my heart and held me rigid lost some of its hold. I was given hope again. As for Erik, while he has never returned to the person he used to be, his eyes now danced and responded once again. I remember well the sweet pain that filled my heart one night not long after the issue of Erik's future had been settled. I was lying in bed, ready to sleep, when I heard Erik murmuring and talking to himself with a tired, satisfied, happy sound. Tears trickled down my cheeks as I realized I had not heard him make sounds like this in several years. Every person should have the God-given right to happiness, to experience that tired, contented feeling at the end of the day when you drift off to sleep knowing you have truly lived and not just existed.

The iron band of fear that had surrounded my heart and held me rigid lost some of its hold.

I now serve in an advisory capacity on two government boards and am involved in a wide range of parent advocacy and support organizations. I owe the person I have become to my children, and especially to Erik. He came to me with the total trust that I could fulfill my part in our sacred pact. How could I let him down?

Life has been a journey, one that is not over yet, but one that is filled with endless opportunities for change and evolution. You never know where you will find a mentor. I am lucky to be living with mine.

Just Ashlyn and Me . . . Always Has Been

JESSICA BRIDGES

THE BABY-BOOK DAYS are over.

My daughter has reached the age of six, too old to have her every accomplishment recorded in a diary.

Unlike the experience of many other parents I know, writing in Ashlyn's baby book had always been a chore instead of a delight. Each entry marks a time when I sat down and tried to make her early years sound just like everyone else's, coming up with creative ways to fit "first steps" into the Year Two section and "first sentence" after the "School Days" pages.

Now, as I close the book, I remember how painful the ritual of writing in it used to be. It was all a pretense, I know now, an attempt to document my child according to society's guidelines rather than her own. My daughter grew and her abilities did not. So I pretended. Some day, I thought, some day soon, everything will just fall into place, and Ashlyn and I will find ourselves just like everyone else.

It is just my daughter and me, and always has been. Her father has floated in and out, oblivious to our struggles. I am the one who fights on her behalf, who supports her, who has become her strongest advocate.

Before Ashlyn, I was never the tough one. Now the woman who once couldn't stand up for herself can confidently argue with medical experts and battle with insurance companies and school districts. Confident in the knowledge that I know better than anyone else what my daughter is capable of, I have found the drive to keep pushing and insisting until we get the results we want.

What got me to this point? I have no idea. All I know is that somewhere in me there was a fighter, and my daughter found her. Ashlyn has turned me into the person I am. Through her special needs I have found a new side of myself. I used to be self-conscious, always comparing myself to others. I used to wonder what other people were thinking about my life, what they thought about the way I raised a special-needs child on my own.

There were days when I would emotionally sit through doctor's appointments or school evaluations and think that the people behind those desks probably pitied me and the lack of a wedding ring on my finger. I have never wanted pity and am more than happy with the life my daughter and I have together. Yes, it has been extremely hard to fight for her on my own, and it probably always will be. But I will continue to do it because I know that I can.

On Ashlyn's first day of kindergarten I made the decision to never compare her to another child again. She is her own person and has the right to be treated as a unique individual, especially by her mother. I refuse to look at what others her age are doing or where she should be by now. Where she should be is exactly where she is and that is what I will concentrate on for the rest of my life.

There is a reason that God gave me Ashlyn. Maybe it was to help me find my own strength. If so, the plan worked.

I have heard it said that if you tell yourself something for long enough, you come to believe it. This has happened to me. I have always told myself that Ashlyn will get somewhere, even when others have said she would not. I watch her go through her days, the toughest little person I have ever seen, and I am in awe of her own confidence. In watching her, I have grown too.

Today I can bear to see there are still blank pages in Ashlyn's book. I can sit down with my daughter and read it to her, laughing about the silly ways she found to get around or the funny sounds she made to communicate her needs. Now I can spend my days with my daughter enjoying her. She is the most precious thing I have.

I am confident in the mother I have become and in the life I am able to give her. I do not wait for the day someone will come along and make us the picture-perfect family. Instead I enjoy the family we are and I enjoy the child that she is. I do not question why God gave us the life we have because, in Ashlyn's eyes, it is perfect.

And those are the eyes that count.

Learn to Be Still

PAM GROSS

I STARTED TASTING fear as soon as I heard the doctor say our baby had developed an irregular heartbeat.

Acid churned in my stomach and terror gripped my heart. I was twenty-six weeks along in my pregnancy, had previously miscarried three times in four years, and at the age of forty-one I knew this was my last chance at motherhood. I traveled to a specialist every other day, dreading what he might tell me, until the irregular heartbeat mysteriously disappeared ten days later. As I listened to the baby's strong, galloping heartbeat, I breathed a huge sigh of relief and hoped the rest of the pregnancy would be uneventful.

Our son was born three months later during a harvest moon. The acute fear that had enveloped me earlier had never really left. Rather, it had become a nagging, ever-present "what if?" lurking in the back of my mind. It was this persistent unease that had convinced me to give birth in one of Georgia's best neonatal hospitals, a decision that was to serve our family very well indeed.

As I had feared, there was indeed something wrong with my baby. Born with Down syndrome, my son had severe breathing problems immediately after birth and was taken to intensive care. Terror once again enveloped me, only this time it was almost mind-numbing.

In the shock that surrounded his first forty-eight hours, concern for my son's life had completely overshadowed the diagnosis of Down syndrome.

Later, however, when he was out of danger and my initial concern had dissipated, the need to concentrate on his disability became my driving force in life. I read books, did research, joined support groups, and started our baby in physical, occupational, speech, aquatic, and music therapy. I was dubbed "therapy mom," and many other mothers of children with Down syndrome contacted me for advice.

I'd heard that knowledge was power; I thought this was a way of gaining some power over my fear. I thought wrong. During out son's annual checkup at the cardiologist's office, I was told he had a problem with one of the valves in his heart and would require open-heart surgery within four years. As I choked down that vaguely familiar acidic taste of fear, I began to contemplate once again the fragility of life. What did the future have in store for us?

Apart from the news of his impending surgery, all my painstaking research had alerted me to the fact that children with Down syndrome have a higher probability of serious health problems such as leukemia. Suddenly the "knowledge equals power" adage just wasn't adding up. Knowledge didn't give you power over fear; it just brought new fears with it.

As a self-confessed "therapy mom," I had long been apprehensive about the support and intervention services my baby was receiving. At a meeting with an early-intervention specialist who was evaluating our son's eligibility for a new government-funded intervention program, I suddenly realized that my misgivings were well founded. Put simply, we were told our child wasn't eligible for the program because, despite being evaluated as having gross and fine motor skills delays, the delays were not significant enough.

At that point apprehension turned into blistering, red-hot rage. Just who in the hell was this so-called specialist? She had spent a mere hour asking questions about our son and had basically disregarded the reports from other therapists. From fear and anger, I quickly moved on to advocacy. I insisted our child remain eligible to receive the therapies in questions and took the issue immediately to the head representative of our district. A resolution was negotiated.

Slowly I was learning that fear does not have to be a paralyzing emotion. Directed the right way, it can be an invaluable guide.

Fear had helped me to the right decision about the hospital I chose to deliver our baby. Fear had taught me that life is precious and that we should appreciate each and every moment. Fear had turned me into an effective advocate. I might not be able to live my life without fear, but I would no longer allow fear to control my life.

Please don't misunderstand me. I still have and will always have concerns for our child. I've been worried about our education system falling short of his needs. I've been afraid that other children will make fun of our son's differences, because sometimes kids can be cruel. I've been frightened there may be a lack of community support for our son after my husband and I have died.

So I've decided to let my fear be my guide. I attend conferences, I read material, and I've consulted an attorney about advocating for our child's education. I've raised our son to know God's love, our love, and also self-love. It is my hope that his strong self-esteem can withstand taunts of ignorance from other children. I've ensured the laying of community foundations with an extended group of family, friends, and church members in addition to a guardian and trust fund.

I've attempted to assuage my fears by using them for our own good. It is in this way that I've learned to be still.

Discovering Our Potential

Tara Demers

You were born today, April 26, 2000. You weighed in at nine pounds, nine ounces. We are at the Grey Nuns Hospital, Room 3244. Thank you for entering my life, Kennedy Elaine Demers.

Love, Mommy.

As I started writing on the crisp white paper of my newborn's journal, I thought about the future my daughter and I would share. I felt so ready to face that future. I knew having Kennedy was a good thing.

Throughout my entire pregnancy I had worried that something was going to be wrong with my baby. Now I can smile as I remember how, at her birth just a few hours ago, I was so anxious that something would go wrong. "Is she all right?" I had asked the nurse frantically.

"She's perfect," was the response.

As I wait outside the University of Alberta neonatal intensive care unit, I battle to clear my head of a thousand thoughts and my eyes of their constant flow of tears. I feel their warm wetness trickle down my face. I use my sweater sleeve to wipe them away, only for more to fall in their place. When I stand up, I still feel slightly sore. It has been two days since my perfect baby was born and now she is here, in the intensive care unit, with all the sickest babies in Alberta. I feel sick now. I look for a garbage can, just in case.

I am holding Kennedy's car seat. She should be in here, I think to myself. Instead it is full of congratulation cards and new pink outfits.

> Kennedy, my dear, you are now four days old. Oh my God, I am bawling, I don't know how much stronger I can be. You are so big compared to all the other babies here. Some of these babies are so sick. You are on life support. You are going to have surgery tomorrow. They aren't sure if you can hold on till then. Please do. Together we can get through this!
>
> Love, Mommy.

I am sitting in a quiet room when I hear a lady crying. They say there is no greater loss than the loss of a child. I feel shivers all over.

I decide to go see my daughter. There is a commotion among the nurses as I walk by; they hush each other into strained silence. I pass by Ruth, the smallest baby I have ever seen. She is segregated from the rest of the room by a stark white room divider. I have never known a baby who has died before.

I walk over to Kennedy and talk with her nurse. They have called in a team from Calgary to do her surgery today. They don't believe she will last another day without it. I make all the calls I need to make and try not to think too much.

> Kennedy, today you are three weeks old. Today you got your stitches out and you're eating a little bit too. They say if you can eat two ounces and keep it down, we will be able to take you home on an hour and a half schedule.
>
> Your sweat test for cystic fibrosis came back positive. That's okay. Mommy will read up about it. You are the only black person in Alberta to have CF. You beat the odds, baby.

I am so glad to have Kennedy home, but she is very hard to deal with. Last night she cried for twelve hours straight. I even took her to the emergency room thinking something was wrong. When I tried to talk to the doctor, all that came out were sobs. I'm sleep deprived and yet I hate going to bed at night because I know that soon enough, no matter how exhausted I feel, no matter how depressed I am, Kennedy will start crying again and again. All I can do is hold her tight and cry right along with my daughter.

To write all of this has been difficult for me. It has brought up many old feelings and situations that I wish I could simply forget.

But the writing has also made me realize how much I have changed, how having Kennedy has altered my outlook and my ambitions forever.

My family had always been healthy and we had never had to deal with death too much. Nothing really traumatic had ever happened to me before Kennedy. She has taught me resilience and the real meaning of selflessness. She gave me a new purpose: to take care of my daughter the very best way I could. Even though her life may be shortened by half, I need to make it a good life. My daughter is more than a medical term. More than a disability.

Once I discovered the potential in Kennedy, I somehow found a little in myself.

Once I discovered the potential in Kennedy, I somehow found a little in myself as well. I have decided to go back to school and I am currently studying social work. Once I graduate, I have dreams of working with parents and children in a hospital setting.

I want to be able to share my story with others. I want those in crisis to know that I understand how it feels and to take comfort in knowing that I have once been where they are now. I am willing to risk showing myself to others, and I have Kennedy to thank for that.

Never Staying Quiet

Tina Rivenbark

My son was born in 1985, three weeks earlier than expected. He came out of the blue, not breathing, and spent the first three hours of his life in intensive care. Once they had stabilized him, the medical staff said he was perfectly normal.

To be quite honest, until he was around thirteen months old, he appeared to be a perfect baby. He only cried when he was hurt, sick, or hungry. All the milestones came early—he walked at nine months, spoke words at ten months, spoke sentences at fifteen months. Before he was two years of age, my boy could recognize letters and numbers and could faithfully repeat things he heard on TV. Then there were the odd things he would do: spinning the bike tires rather than riding the bike itself, preferring his own company to that of other children.

By the time he was four years old and ready for preschool, he was already reading at a fourth-grade level. However, he did not have any self-help skills and still made no effort to make friends. He insisted on having his own way constantly and resorted to violent tantrums to ensure that he achieved that end.

In the early years I kept telling my husband that something was not right about our son. He would not hear of such things. Our son was a gifted little professor in my hubby's eyes, and that was the end of the matter.

Well, all my fears were confirmed when, at the age of four, he was kicked out of preschool. The preschool staff told me to have him tested, and I spent the next four years doing just that, frantically searching for the diagnosis that would solve the puzzle of my child.

In those years I went to so many doctors, I lost count. I was advised to do everything from attending parenting classes to giving my son Ritalin. One "expert" even suggested that the fault lay in my failure to breast-feed: my son had not been properly nurtured and therefore I had not bonded with him. Needless to say, while the specialists dithered, I got so angry that I just wanted to scream. And many times I did!

My son just kept growing up. His self-help skills did not improve, nor did his need to have friends. I decided at one point that I could teach him to make friends by bringing a constant stream of children into our home. I started a baby-sitting service and watched as he drove all the other children crazy, including his younger brother.

At age eight he had been expelled from a private school and was having an unhappy time within the public school system. On the one hand he was very bright, but his peculiar behaviors were a complete mystery to everyone. His strange ways had left him alienated from both his peers, who teased him constantly, and his teachers, who found his "bad" behavior a constant source of irritation. The calls of complaint from the school became a constant in my life.

At my wit's end, I made the bold decision to home-school him. I'd had enough of bad advice from medical professionals and educators. At the same time I began an intense search to find a name for the problems that had caused my son and our family so much pain.

To make a long story short, I did succeed in finding a name for what my son had: high-functioning autism, also known as Asperger's syndrome. Once we had a diagnosis, it was suggested to me that my boy could possibly go back to school if an individual education plan (IEP) was formulated to suit his needs.

Full of hope, I approached our local school district and requested that an IEP be developed. Incredibly, it took a considerable amount of time and a rather large payment to a lawyer specializing in education law to win that particular battle. With an IQ of 118 and a syndrome that few people had ever heard of, it took the threat of legal action to make the school district realize that our son actually did need help.

Although we did get that IEP in the long run, the whole incident marked a very stressful time in our lives. Realizing I needed support, I contacted the Autism Society about finding a local support group for parents. There were none. Undeterred, I decided that if I could not go to the mountain, the mountain could come to me. I founded the North Central Ohio Chapter of the Autism Society and in doing so found a way to turn my anger into positive energy. I sent every person who had misdiagnosed my son an information pack. I forced the schools to attend autism seminars. I was a very busy and determined beaver. Thanks to our efforts, our son got two years of individualized, quality schooling that we will always treasure.

All good things must end. Life, after all, is ever changing. After a while the time came for my son to start junior high, and the struggles began all over again. The fight with the schools returned . . . *ding, ding,* round two.

This time the local school district presented me with a number of educational options and I did my best to assess them all as objectively as possible. It was when they suggested he attend a special school for children with drug- and alcohol-related behavioral problems that I realized I had in fact only two options: I could go the legal route once more, or simply return to home schooling him. Tired of battle and unsure of the chances of victory, I decided to educate my son myself once again.

My boy is now sixteen and still being taught at home, but this time with a pleasing twist. He is enrolled in an Electronic Classroom of Tomorrow program (ECOT). The state of Ohio provides him with a computer and a fax/printer and he is schooled via the Internet. He has an IEP and a wonderful special education teacher who actually understands autism. He has a summer job and does volunteer work during the school year for his work-study program. He's not ready to drive, but he thinks he might want to some day.

I no longer run the autism chapter, but it's still going strong, with meetings averaging thirty people a month. The kids in our community who are diagnosed with Asperger's syndrome are now getting the help they need much faster than my son. We spoke before the school board this past summer and were very well received.

Things are changing very slowly in our area for kids like my son. But they are changing . . . and I intend never to stay quiet on the topic of autism.

Marriage, Family, and Friends

Life has taught us that love does not consist in
   gazing at each other,
But in looking outward together in
   the same direction.

ANTOINE DE SAINT-EXUPÉRY

Introduction

Neil Nicoll

Family life in the twenty-first century is both a challenge and a richly rewarding experience. When a family also includes a child with a disability, the challenges are most certainly heightened, but so, too, are the rewards.

Accepting that your family life will include both moments of intense anguish and moments of great joy is a major step toward coming to terms with caring for a child with a disability. The family unit will almost certainly be tested with the arrival of a special-needs child, but it can also become stronger as well.

The Myth of the "Perfect" Family

There are no perfect families. I know this for a fact because a perfect family would need to be made up of perfect people, and I have never come across a single one of those either.

Every family has its own idiosyncrasies, its own secrets, its own unique and sometimes—to the outside observer—even odd ways of doing things. Families with disabled children are certainly no different in this regard.

Strangely, however, there remains an idealized view of the relationships within those families with special-needs children. The myth—and it surely is that—says that the members of such a family bond more closely together as a result of the child; that such parents become smarter, more patient, and more philosophical about life; and that siblings enjoy lavishing attention on their "special" brother or sister.

While it is true that some families do some of these things some of the time, there is no guarantee that caring for a child with a disability will result in personal growth of this nature. Allow your family to be what it is rather than what you think it should be.

Staying Together

Caring for a child with a disability can be extremely stressful, and under such conditions interpersonal relationships can suffer. While the child is seldom the key factor in the decision for parents to divorce, the additional strain of meeting the child's special needs often plays some role in marital breakdowns.

Allow your family to be what it is rather than what you think it should be.

Previous chapters have discussed the grieving process in relation to loss, and to disability, and it is worth reiterating that no two people grieve or adjust to loss in the same way. This in itself may be a source of tension within families as partners (and other family members) endeavor to deal with their own grief, while at the same time trying to support their partner. If the parents have a markedly different grieving style, conflict and misunderstanding can quickly result. For instance, if one parent is immersed in guilt over the birth of a disabled child while the other is deep in a denial/anger pattern, a highly charged emotional environment could result. Combine this dilemma with the very real need for parents to develop skills and strategies for caring for their child, and you have a setting hostile to the positive growth of family relationships.

Another challenge for modern family life is that of rules and expectations in relation to behavior and responsibilities. Family members may interpret these quite differently and may communicate differing expectations to their children, creating another source of conflict and stress. If both parents work, which one of them should take the most time off work for the child's regular medical appointments? If someone has to give up work to care for the child full-time, who should that be? How much responsibility should the child's older siblings take in terms of caring for their brother or sister and helping out their parents? Shouldn't Grandma come and baby-sit more often; don't Mom and Dad really need a regular break from the kids? How these specific issues are managed can have a dramatic influence on the peace and harmony of family life.

Yet another hurdle for families to overcome is that of "loss" of previous lifestyles and opportunities. All couples experience significant changes to lifestyle when they have children, if only because they rapidly become too busy to do all the things they used to do. Again, when a family has a child with a disability, there is usually an even greater loss of freedom in this respect. Life becomes extremely busy with a range of appointments to keep, therapies to learn and apply, and behavioral and logistical challenges to meet. Parents may feel they have far less time for themselves, their relatives and friends than they ever thought possible.

They often feel too exhausted to participate in social activities, or simply feel overwhelmed by the logistical difficulties associated with going to the movies, a restaurant, or a party with their child. Hobbies become neglected and friendships are let go of. Some parents feel that their world is shrinking. Even their contacts with other adults may be confined to parents of other children with disabilities whom they have met through school or support groups. It can take a very determined parent to maintain a sense of balance and normality in their life, but the benefits of doing so are enormous.

Children with disabilities vary greatly in their needs and in the intensity of care required. Their care often involves additional duties and expertise that would not have to be considered in the context of a non-disabled child. Sharing these tasks—especially if they are unpleasant or emotionally stressful—must be done as equitably as possible. Complaints that one partner does not pulling his or her weight can lead to more significant resentment building up over time.

Sibling Issues

If it's hard being the parent of a child with disabilities, why do so many people assume that being that child's brother or sister to the same child is any less taxing? The siblings of disabled children have a great many additional burdens placed on their shoulders, but their needs are often neglected and seldom discussed.

Other children within the family experience grief and loss just like the grown-ups do. They may have lost a playmate and a friend. They may have lost extra attention from their parents. For some it may be the loss of friendships as other children stay away through fear, ignorance, or embarrassment.

Some siblings may experience an even greater loss—the loss of childhood. Required to take on extra responsibility because of the extra burden placed on the family by the disabled siblings, some children become virtual supplementary parents at a time in their lives when other children are relatively carefree.

Of course, it's not all bad news for siblings. Far from it! Many develop enormous patience and learn to embrace diversity, traits that will stand them in good stead later in life. Some, however, can become quite bitter and jealous at the perceived disparity in attention given to them compared to this disabled sibling. Others can become very embarrassed if the sibling regularly displays challenging behaviors in public, while in extreme cases a child may be quite traumatized by a particularly aggressive brother or sister.

For all these reasons, it is important to consider your non-disabled children within the family structure. Make special time for them whenever possible. Respite care is available to many parents and should be seen as an opportunity not only for parents to enjoy themselves but for your other children to do so as well. Catch a movie, walk in the park, go out to lunch—what you do isn't nearly as important as the fact that you do it together.

The Extended Family

A family usually consists of more than just a mother, father, and children. For most of us, grandparents, cousins, uncles and aunts, and parents-in-law are all part of the family picture to varying degrees. These people will have their own reactions to disability, and their input can have a significant impact on how the family deals with the arrival of a "special" new member.

Grandparents are often an enormous source of strength and support for parents. They can offer emotional support and comfort, act as baby-sitters and respite caregivers, and generally provide invaluable backup to parents.

On the other hand, grandparents—and indeed other relatives and close friends—can provide parents with some challenges of their own. Questioning or even disagreeing with diagnoses, arguing about the right or wrong way to manage the child's condition, scolding one parent for not helping the other out enough—these are the sorts of interventions that parents can usually do without.

In most cases, a combative friend or relative is usually experiencing denial or some form of grief in relation to the disabled child. Usually, as the grief fades, so too do the arguments. Patience and a little understanding on the part of the parent can often head off disputes before they become too acrimonious. Occasionally, however, differences can be irreconcilable. When this happens, parents have little choice but to face the reality that their relationship with other family members or friends may have changed dramatically and, possibly, permanently.

In times of crisis you find out who your real friends are. Some parents find that the reason their social circle shrinks after the birth of their child is because they themselves become far more selective and critical of the people they let into their lives. Time can become too precious to continue unproductive or nonsupportive relationships. Estrangement from one group of friends or relatives is often compensated for by the development of new relationships with people more willing to see the world from your new perspective.

We Take Nothing for Granted

Carolyn Fennell

AFTER NEARLY TWO YEARS of being told there was nothing wrong with our son, we were told quite abruptly that, yes, there seemed to be a problem.

He had been born two years after our daughter, and as a mother you just know there is something amiss. He was a beautiful baby, but he suffered almost monthly from ear infections. At fourteen months, when his speech ceased developing and bad behavior took its place, I began to really worry. Countless phone calls, visits to doctors, therapists, and any other current "miracle workers" was how I filled my days.

After several months I realized that all I had been doing was looking for someone to cure my son, when in reality the professionals I was seeing had no clue as to why our son was like this or what to call the condition. I had to make choices about the best places for him to be taught, not only language but also social and behavioral skills.

I have been enormously lucky with those choices, partly because of the help I received from people I met along the way who also had children with developmental problems. The friendships that have formed for my husband and me are unique, and the friendships that exist for our son are invaluable.

Having a child in a mainstream school environment and one at a special school is sometimes difficult. It never seems fair that our children can't go to school together, that our daughter can't look out for her little brother as she would so much want to do.

Our son's school is a very nurturing place where the children have a wide variety of needs. He loves going there and has come such a long way with all his learning skills. It is also a safe haven for our family. We can attend school functions and activities knowing there is always going to be a relaxed approach to whatever the children do, whereas under other circumstances it can be upsetting to see how hard the children try to accomplish things that so many take for granted.

I guess my journey through all this has made me stronger. I choose not to look any farther down the track than six months because it would be too hard. The nine years since having our son have been completely life-changing. At first I believed that any normality was out of the question. We had to choose very carefully where we went, who we went with, and how they would be with our son. That put pressure on all of us because we couldn't ignore the fact that our daughter wanted a normal life doing things that we did prior to her brother's arrival. We soon learned that staying home was the easiest option for us—that is, until he started school at age five. Going places he was unfamiliar with was always hard, and even now he needs to know where we are going and likes to be told repeatedly. The comforting thing about that is that now he is interested and usually excited by our outings.

We are so lucky that our son has no health issues associated with his condition. We are enormously proud of what a lovely boy he is turning out to be and what a great sense of humor he is developing. He is very good with routine, and that keeps us all on an even keel. In a lot of ways the behavior we have found challenging has proven to be normal when we witness the same in our friend's boy, and that is reassuring.

I am very sad when I think how many times I attributed his behavior to his problem and failed to deal with it in a "normal" way. Never knowing the diagnosis or prognosis for our son has been difficult, not because we require a "label" for him but just so that we have a guideline as to what to expect in the future.

When I became a parent, I experienced a whole new range of emotions, but when presented with the role of caring and nurturing a "special" child, I seemed to acquire so much more. I feel really unique, because my son himself is so unique. Our family takes nothing for granted, and we all feel an enormous sense of protectiveness where he is concerned. No parent can be sure of their child's future, but I really feel that our son will progress and surpass our hopes. Even at age nine he can work out video games that his dad has trouble understanding. It's almost as if he is keeping his capabilities a secret.

What People Say . . .

SHARON PERERA

JOSHIE IS MY SON—our son actually, Andrew's and mine—and he is Emily's brother. All of us love him very much, love him fiercely, all the more so because of his disability—and yet it seems that we go through life listening to other people's opinions about our boy.

I started to notice that something was amiss with Joshie when he was two months old. However, the people I spoke to convinced me his brief epileptic spasms were due to "trapped wind." It didn't take much to convince me. But the nagging feeling didn't go away, and as he grew older, the spasms became more noticeable. On three occasions I went to my GP to tell him about my fears. On the first two occasions he looked Joshie over and I was out the door in five minutes. The third time I was there, I brought up the question of petit mal (minor absences). My GP blustered some more and then told me about the hazards of "reading too much literature." It was quite a while before I managed to convince anyone that my son wasn't right.

On his first birthday Joshie was diagnosed with tuberous sclerosis. I remember the specialist asking my husband and me if we could go somewhere quiet, and I remember the sinking feeling that it couldn't be good news if it had to be a private room. I should have taken comfort at her reassurances that Joshie would have a normal life expectancy, but what kept on clanging in my mind was that his condition was incurable. I felt at that moment that my life ceased to be worth living. I didn't believe I could ever be happy again. My beautiful, precious family was no longer. We were disabled, spoiled, destroyed. A lifetime of disability was all I could think about.

We hobbled through the following year, trying out different schools, seeing experts, searching for peace of mind in the knowledge that we were doing the right thing by Joshie—that he was being provided for. But the deep-seated unhappiness never left me. I could never talk about it, not even to my own husband. Doing so would be to deepen already raw wounds, and I was tired of thinking and talking about it.

But one day, when Joshie was about two years old, on our way to one of his therapy sessions, the taxi driver who was taking us there recognized the Center for Disabled Children. He told me about his own twelve-year-old son who was also disabled. In our mutual sadness, I suddenly said to this complete stranger that I didn't think I could ever be happy again. I don't even know what he looked like, because he was driving at the time, but he replied stoically that we couldn't change the situation. "We just need to do what we can, we can't do more than that."

We still have our difficult moments. We argue and get cross when we feel stretched and tired.

If this had been a movie, the music would have blared out at this moment, because to me it was a revelation. I had been trying to cover all corners, to give Joshie everything that was out there. I was trying to be all that I thought I had to be. His simple comment showed me that it wasn't possible—there, in the taxi, I was relieved of my burden of guilt and frustration; and I glimpsed peace.

I've thought about it a lot since then. In those early times I couldn't see that I still had my beautiful family. Worse still, I had been neglecting my daughter. Although she'd never complained, and loved her brother as selflessly as I did, she too was growing up. All the time I'd been worrying about Joshie, she was missing out on things I could have done with her, things we could have done together with Joshie.

We still have our difficult moments. We argue and get cross when we feel stretched and tired. We are frustrated by the constraints around us. We think long and hard about family outings.

We can't leave the children with a babysitter for a short weekend break (I have no family living nearby), and Joshie never gets invited to friends' houses or birthday parties. At Christmas I overheard nine-year-old Emily talking to her twenty-six-year-old cousin—"What in the world would you wish for for Christmas?" was the topic of conversation.

"I'd wish to could go to Australia for a long holiday" was the cousin's reply.

"I'd wish that Joshie was normal like me" was my daughter's wish.

But, as always, the taxi driver's words rang true—we can't change things, we can only do what we are able to do. In all our troubles, and in the many countries where we've lived, we've received support from the most surprising places, much of which has been invaluable to my family. And yet, oftentimes, we find it a hard society that we live in, regardless of which country we are in.

People, in their embarrassed way of showing me support, tell me that they don't know if they could cope as I do in the same situation I'm in, but that's nonsense. It isn't a noble thing I'm doing; I didn't set out to have a disabled child to prove what a strong person I can be. People say that all Joshie's progress is due to what a good parent I am. Yet they don't tell me the same thing about Emily. People want to have something to say because they're uncomfortable about what to say, I guess. I forgive them for that.

But some things are harder to forgive. On the other end of the scale, people think they're helping when they dish out advice glibly: Children like that need to do horse riding, it helps them to look ahead; children like that should be given frogs' legs to eat, it'll help them walk more normally. More cruel still are the comments Emily gets from other children: "Why does your brother walk in that way?" or "Your brother does weird things."

Perhaps the most astounding thing I've heard yet is from a psychologist. In his learned opinion, Joshie has long spells of laughter because it's his defense against an unpleasant situation! (I think he laughs when he's amused and then can't stop laughing, as many of us do from time to time.)

I could tell you that Joshie is a treasured gift and that his angelic innocence is unique. That he is our lesson in love, faith, humility, patience . . . and hope. Some of these things people have told us. Some of these things we say to ourselves. All of them are true. It's a long, long journey of discovery and rediscovery, of setting and resetting goals.

I have come to realize that I can't live my life in pursuit of the ideal arrangement. Instead I accept my family as they are and gratefully experience every new day with them—enjoying most of them, getting through others.

Pride, Love, and a Whole Lot to Be Learned

Lisa Depperman

I FIRST NOTICED the stares at the mall when Mason was an infant. Two older ladies were walking, and when they saw him in his stroller, they gave first him, then me, looks of disgust. I told my friend, who was with me at the time, to watch people look at him. At first she said I was imagining things, but as we walked on, she too began to notice. The looks clearly said, "How could you bring such a child into the world?" The anger overwhelmed me, and I thought to myself, "Why do you criticize me?" Did I have a choice with my disabled child? Then I realized that I should not judge what others might be thinking, for I have not lived their lives.

I believe that it was that encounter and similar ones that followed that changed my philosophy and me forever. I came to realize that there is no shame in having a child with Down syndrome or any disability. There is only pride, love, and a whole lot to be learned and to teach others. So from that day forward we went out into the world and lived life as a complete family, one that would only be seen with all its members present. To playgroups, to church, to the park, and to the mall we would go with our heads held high, no tears in my eyes. No strangers in the mall would make me cry for my child again, for I was ready to teach the world a thing or two!

It helps immensely that both of my children are outgoing and never had any problems letting the world know they exist and are proud of it. Going to the park would become routine for us, and when Casi wanted to meet someone, she would simply introduce herself along with Mason. "And this is my brother, Mason. He's four and he has Down syndrome."

Or at a school talent show, when she got up in front of an audience and proclaimed that because her brother has Down syndrome and does not learn as fast as other kids, we had to learn sign language and that she was going to perform a song in sign. How could a mother not be filled with joy and pride over both her children, when there was not a dry eye in the place?

But, every once in a while, the fears would come back. In new situations I'd wonder if the stares would return and if we would be discriminated against the way we had a few times before. I found the thought of sending Mason to school a particularly daunting one since I was not too familiar with the system, the laws of the people. As any parent can understand, I worried that he would be teased or just plain excluded. How could I help when I was not going to be there the way I always had in the past? I did not want Casi to carry the burden, but I must admit I was totally relieved that she was there.

But to school he went, a state of affairs that to this day I cannot agree with. Why would I send my child, who was developmentally delayed and the size of a three-year-old, to school at the age of five, when I would not send my typical child to school until she was age six? The law, I was told, does not force you to send your child to school until he is six, but the school does not have to provide services if he is five and not enrolled in kindergarten. Not being able to afford his numerous and necessary therapies, we were left with no choice. That was one of the many battles I have tried to fight, and lost, but there are so many to be fought in a lifetime that there will also be many wins.

School has matured Mason to a degree, but it is the adults and the other children who have really changed. Since Mason started at his school, I have seen staff who have not been known to smile or be loving, be very loving and happy with Mason. Numerous people have told me how wonderful it is to have him and how lucky we all are to be in his life. Although this makes me feel wonderful as his mother, I feel a tinge of sadness at the same time. This sadness is not just for Mason and our family, but for all the children and families living with special needs. Do we prejudge each other so quickly that we assign a stigma or a set of circumstances based on looks or what *we* think? I am embarrassed to admit that even after Mason was born, in my anger at the world, I hated to look at other moms with their "perfect" children and see their happiness. I prejudged so badly that one day at the park I watched three pretty moms with their group of "perfect" children and thought, "Isn't that nice—witches!," only to meet them and get to know them and the suffering of one woman's dying mother and another whose son was autistic. I do not want others to judge Mason, Casi, my husband or me, but somehow, up until then, I had managed to judge others.

Then, as many times in life, it comes back to the children themselves. A colleague of mine came to me at work and told me that she wanted to share a story with me. She said that she and her son, Scotty, who is in the fifth grade in the same school as Mason, were having a conversation about people with disabilities. She said that Scotty had asked her if she knew anyone with a disability. She replied that, yes, in fact there was a boy at his school who had Down syndrome. Scotty asked who. She said, "The boy in the kindergarten class." He said, "The Oriental boy?" She went on to explain that that was actually a feature of Down syndrome. Scotty replied, "No Mom, that boy is perfect." His mother asked, "What do you mean?" Scotty replied, "He's perfect, Mom, he is always happy and smiling and never angry."

So to the mall we go and everywhere else, with pride, with joy, and at times a feeling that anyone can have a typical child, but not everyone can have a "perfect" one.

Much to Be Thankful For

Barbara Bucknam

Yes, it is emotionally painful to have a child with autism. I can handle it one day at a time, not looking too far into the future, or so I thought. Everything changed on the morning of September 11, 2001. On that day I thought my worst nightmare had come true; I thought I might have become a single parent. I don't know how a single parent can raise an autistic child on his or her own. I know there are many single parents of autistic children, and I truly respect them for the difficult job they are doing. I personally don't know if I could find the strength to carry on without my husband sharing in this role.

On that historic day, while out running errands, my life went into slow motion after I heard on my car radio that a plane had hit the Pentagon where my air force fighter-pilot husband works. I spoke to him twice that morning after the World Trade Center strikes. I frantically tried to call him again, but all the lines were busy. I pulled off the road, trying to cope with my wild, racing thoughts, "The Pentagon can't be completely destroyed. It is a really big building, one plane can't demolish it all, can it? Please, God, don't let him be in pain. Am I a widow now? Do we really have enough life insurance? We haven't signed our revocable trusts yet." And last but not least, "Don't get into a car accident yourself!"

After a few deep breaths (can you spell *h-y-p-e-r-v-e-n-t-i-l-a-t-e*?) and a distressed phone call to my sister, I carefully drove home to my five-year-old autistic son and his therapist, who were oblivious of the catastrophic world events that had just been unleashed. I was never so happy to see a blinking red light on my telephone answering machine and I have yet to erase the reassuring message from my husband, "Honey, I'm fine."

Somehow autism isn't quite so hard to face now. It's been over five years since the initial diagnosis was confirmed. We've learned to adjust, to accept, and to come to terms with our son's limitations. There are still two of us to spread the load of caring for him. We can exchange ideas, discuss how to handle some new behavior, savor a milestone reached, and jointly ponder the uncertain future of our son (though, as I know so well, none of our futures are certain).

Beyond our son, my main concern has been worrying over how autism in the family affects our eldest child, our eight-year-old daughter. What is her genetic risk for bearing an autistic child? Will she want a relationship with her brother when they are both adults? I do not want her to be solely responsible for her brother after we have gone, assuming he is able to lead an independent life. Yet how can that be avoided since she is the only sibling? Mostly I want her to grow up as normally as possible (hah!) and not have to live in a home full of stress where everything centers around autism.

I look forward to the day when anger is no longer the number-one emotion she feels toward her brother, and he says "I love you" to her without being verbally prompted to do so.

Since that eventful day in September, spending time together is vastly more important to me. Watching a tear come to my macho husband's eye while he listened to our precious little boy recite the Pledge of Allegiance for the first time on Veterans Day is a memory I will hold deep in my heart, especially when autism gets to be more than I think I can handle for that day. We grin fondly now when our son says the entire pledge anytime he sees a flag—and they are quite prominently on display these days.

Our family has so much to be thankful for: Our children have a normal life expectancy, they are free from any terminal disease, major accidents have not befallen us, so far we have the resources to pay for our son's various therapies, and our son will never grow up to be a terrorist who wreaks havoc, destroying precious human life. Though the challenges of autism are at times daunting, many of them are temporary and mild compared to other life-shattering events. It is all in your perspective.

OPOs—Other People's Opinions

Gracie Mackay

WHEN YOU ARE PREGNANT with a child, something whispers in the back of your mind: "Have I done everything right?" "Will there be anything wrong?" Then when the child is born the voice asks, "Is he breathing? Are all the limbs there?" All postnatal checks are okay. An angry, red, slimy bundle of fury is placed in your arms. You instinctively hold the creature to your breast, vowing without conscious recognition that you will protect and care for it as long as you live. Three years later you are tearing your hair out, crying constantly from the fatigue that seeps through your body like poison, staring helplessly at this creature born of your loin. What went wrong?

It took seven more years to find the answer.

In the meantime we had a child who was a cross between an angelic genius and the devil reincarnate. It wasn't really until my son started going to school that we realized there was more to this child than simply a personality difference, but it was many years into his schooling before we found the answers we needed. Until we found those answers we struggled with OPOs: other people's opinions. OPOs come in many shapes and forms: some sympathetic ("You poor dear, being burdened with *that*"), some accusatory ("If you would *discipline* that child occasionally . . ."), and some downright obnoxious ("You and your son are ****.") Add whatever comes to mind.

The professionals have OPOs, too. One diagnosed "overprotective parenting" which was probably designed to make us sit back in our rightful place and think, "Of course, it's our fault!"

When he turned three, I enrolled my son in Montessori Kinder, as much for my sanity as for his well-being. He had become a dis-assembler, a destroyer of all around him, and needed new horizons to keep his ever-active mind entertained; I needed some peace. Knowing full well that I was sending him off in part to help myself was hard—all the OPOs of me being a selfish, incapable parent had apparently been justified.

The behavioral problems, idiosyncrasies, and eccentricities increased with the years, and what continues to make this situation worse is that he looks just like anyone else. His is an invisible disability—the ever-present pain and confusion is masked by a "normal" facade.

The hardest times are clear in my mind. There were the times we went to parks as a family and our eldest daughter would make three friends within minutes while her younger brother would make three enemies in the same amount of time, some of whom would be adults. There were the early years when, with a determined, silent face, he would pursue his objective relentlessly until I cried with exhaustion. (He was the second and I was pregnant again.) There were the voices of those we call family who told us that we had failed, and the voices of those we call friends who said the same. Always there was the nagging doubt in the backs of our minds that these people were right. The hardest time of all was also the greatest as it finally led us to answers.

"Have you heard of Asperger's syndrome?" our GP asked, laughing. I was in a deep depression and had gone to him as a last resort. Our son had told the principal he'd been "bashed," and mandatory reporting meant we were to be visited by child-protection authorities. You may wonder why the GP was laughing. I can only guess he wanted to let us know that the accusation was preposterous. By some bizarre twist of fate, this darkest moment was the beginning of our quest to help our son. We started the treadmill of diagnosis, which is never easy, yet all along the way we found answers, reasons, and hope. We learned of the incredible beauty that goes with the difficulties, and that there have been many successful, brilliant, and capable people who have also had an autism spectrum disorder. We learned what to expect (mostly) and started to learn how to deal with our situation. Our boy hadn't been "bashed." His wise principal (who stood by our side regardless of the fact that she had no choice but to report the accusation) suggested we show him a film called *Goodnight, Mr. Tom*, and he saw that the smack he wasn't used to receiving was far removed from child abuse. The scar of this time will remain in my heart forever, a battle wound of motherhood.

We learned something else valuable during this process. We learned that much of his problem had gone unnoticed because he and I view the world in a similar way. Yes, I too have Asperger's syndrome. Relief is the only way to describe the sudden explanation as to why you are on a path that is different from the rest of the crowd.

It wasn't long before our fourth child showed a similar pattern of behavior. This little boy mumbled, found great pleasure in spinning himself on anything at any time, regardless of where he was. This time it wasn't frightening. This time we knew what to look for and what to ask, and we knew that having our suspicions confirmed was a blessing—now he would receive help and, hopefully, understanding. This boy has high-functioning autism, so of our five children, two are on the autistic spectrum.

We are a "different" family, yet we laugh and love and share like anyone else. Our hard times are nothing in comparison to those of a huge percentage of the world, yet a little understanding and acceptance would go a long way toward making our lives, and those of many others in the same position, happier and easier. I prefer the word *difference* to *disability* as there are benefits to be found in any disability, whether it be the one-tracked determination of a boy with Asperger's to develop a new computer program, or the beautiful poetry written by an autistic woman, the compassion of the girl with cystic fibrosis, or the smile of the boy with Down syndrome who makes every waking moment of his mother's life a joy. We are all different, but the closed mind of an able body can be a greater disability than any other.

> *We are a "different" family, yet we laugh and love and share like anyone else.*

On Becoming a Parent

ANDREA CONNELL

M Y FRIENDS AND FAMILY thought I became a parent the day my daughter, Emma, was born. In fact, I thought that was what happened too. I had no idea what the next few months would have in store for Emma, our families, and me.

My name is Andrea. My boyfriend, Cory, and I decided to bring a baby into this world in May 1999. Emma was born in February 2000. She was a much-anticipated baby, being the first great-grandchild. Nine days after she was due, she decided to make her appearance. The delivery went like most, without much complication. Emma did have an eye infection and was jaundiced, but both of these problems cleared up.

Emma was your typical baby, happy as could be. She slept too much, but never at night. She was gaining weight and, as the saying goes, "growing like a weed." Her smiles and coos made the days fly by, and before we knew it, she was two months old and ready for a checkup. Weight and height were good, everything looked fine. Her doctor asked us if she was tracking the bottle yet. I told her, "Not really." Emma always seemed to have busy eyes. I referred to them as "google eyes," the kind you see on dolls whose eyes pop all over. The doctor started shining lights into her eyes and moving things in front of her. She left saying she would be right back. When she finally came back, she told us she had conferred with another doctor and thought Emma should be seen by a pediatric ophthalmologist. My first question was "Why?" What was wrong with my baby? The doctor didn't want to jump to conclusions but thought Emma was having problems seeing. The appointment was made, but it was two weeks away.

I don't think I was in denial, more like shock. My whole family has had eye problems; maybe Emma's just started early. I went back to work and told everyone, and my mom told the rest of my family. There were so many questions whose answers were still two weeks away. After I got off work that night, I took Emma to my room. I started putting my hand in front of her face very quickly and closely to see if she flinched—nothing. I took her toys and moved them all over her face—nothing. I found out later that my whole family had been doing the same thing: we were all trying to find out if Emma could see.

May 10, 2000. I left work to take Emma to the eye doctor with my mom and Cory. They dilated her eyes, shone light in them, and so on. After the doctor examined her, she sat us all down. She told us that Emma had optic nerve hypoplasia. She explained that Emma's eyes were fine, but the nerves that sent information to the brain were much smaller than normal, maybe even nonexistent. Emma was blind.

The rest of the conversation was kind of a blur; I only caught bits and pieces. I didn't like the parts I heard. I was told that there would be special schooling and pretty much that Emma would never be able to do anything. We left in silence. My mom took Emma home, as she watches her while I am at work. I got in the car and cried. I told Cory that our little girl was never going to see how beautiful she was. I begged him to tell me how we would explain colors to her. I wanted answers. I thought of the scrapbook I was making at home. Why finish? Emma would never see it.

As hard as it was, I went back to work that day. I had to keep myself busy. I worked in an office in a hospital. I walked in and saw a little boy in a wheelchair. He was hooked up to machines that were breathing for him, he couldn't move. That is the moment that things began to change. I thought to myself, "At least Emma isn't like that." I realized then that things could be so much worse. When I walked in, everyone wanted to know what happened. It took a long time for me to be able to talk through the tears. No one really knew what to say. I walked over to a girl I was very close with and she cried with me. A girl sitting beside her said something that truly changed the course of how I was going to raise Emma and how I was going to get through this. She said a friend of hers had just had a baby who had Down syndrome. She had been having a rough time with it until someone told her that she was given that baby for a reason. God wanted her to have that baby. At that moment I knew what I was here for. I was put here to help educate people and become an advocate for Emma. God had given me a challenge and I was going to take it.

I must admit this was not an easy challenge, and was going to take some getting used to. I was in the elevator and saw a little baby over its mom's shoulder looking at me. I wanted to yell and scream and tell the baby not to look at me. It wasn't fair that this baby could look at me and my own baby couldn't. There were strangers who would wave at Emma and then say, "Over here," so she would look at them. My heart would ache, but I would have to explain that she couldn't see them.

I got on the Internet and started researching. I found out that Emma's first doctor didn't have a clue about optic nerve hypoplasia. I learned I did nothing wrong in the pregnancy, which put me a little at ease. I remember asking Cory if he was mad at me. He looked at me like I was nuts. He told me it wasn't my fault. I went to all my appointments and took my vitamins religiously. Up until then I thought that I had done something to Emma, which would have broken my heart.

Emma is now two and is doing great. I was under the impression that being blind meant that all you saw was black or white. I learned that Emma can see light, objects, and shadows. I try never to get my hopes up too high but to stay optimistic. I also try to make light of the situation as much as possible. I want people around Emma to feel comfortable and not to think they can't say certain things around her. I remember being at a store and looking for a mirror for my car. I saw some blind-spot mirrors and joked that we could just cover Emma in blind-spot mirrors.

Finally, I would like to go back to the first part of my story. I did not become a parent the day Emma was born. I really became a parent when I heard the words, "Your daughter is blind." I hurt more for Emma than I could have or ever would hurt for myself. In one day I went from anticipation, to heartbreak, to acceptance. I have grown a lot since that day in May. I credit that all to Emma. We have heard a lot about heroes in the past few months [late 2001], and Emma is my hero. She has been through more tests than I will ever go through. Emma is very special to me and to everyone who is in contact with her. Emma has touched so many people's lives, and it is because she is blind. Emma is a very bright girl and will see more than I ever will.

Love and Joy

You may only be one person to the world,
But you may also be the world to one person.

ANONYMOUS

Introduction

NEIL NICOLL

IT IS A RARE PARENT indeed who does not love his or her child. But for parents of disabled children, love often has to jump many hurdles and withstand many blows. It must also battle the societal expectation that raising a disabled child somehow intrinsically makes one more able to cope with grief and stress. Acknowledging your child for who he or she truly is, and refusing to allow others to dictate your behavior are the keys to allowing love to flourish.

> *For parents of disabled children, love often has to jump many hurdles and withstand many blows.*

Ignoring Expectations

Television and movies are very good at placing people in various "character" boxes. Turn on the TV and you'll see characters that are either intrinsically good, or inherently evil, astoundingly clever or stupendously stupid, rich or poor, beautiful or plain. Unlike real life, there are few shades of gray in the fantasy world of films and television.

The disabled and their parents do not escape caricatures either. Overwhelmingly, parents of the disabled are portrayed as little less than saints or martyrs, people endowed with endless patience, love, and compassion and happy to share their poignant insights with others. Such is the impact of the visual media on our lives that such portrayals—patently ridiculous as they may be—sometimes become so widely accepted that even parents themselves feel they have failed to meet some intangible standard of behavior.

Parents are not martyrs. A martyr seeks out his or her fate and wishes to suffer. The parents of disabled children do not choose their role, it is thrust upon them. It is important that parents learn to leave the mythmaking to Hollywood and approach their feelings for their child with honesty and without guilt.

Embracing Reality

If they are being honest, all parents, regardless of whether their child is disabled or not, will admit to times when it has been difficult to love their offspring. Loving a child is not always easy; raising a child is not always a joyful experience. The reality is that most parents have moments—sometimes brief, sometimes prolonged—when they do not like their child very much at all.

For parents of special-needs children still immersed in the fantasy view of their role, this reality can be especially difficult to deal with, and can lead to added feelings of anxiety and stress. After all, society believes them to be some sort of "super parent," and they may feel obliged to live up to expectations.

I have no doubt that parents raising disabled children accomplish great things. But they do so by working harder and longer than other parents, often because they have little choice but to battle on as best they can. Parents need to allow themselves the luxury of getting real about their feelings, of allowing themselves to get angry, to get lazy, to get fed up occasionally—without feeling guilty.

Transition Points

Theorists refer to life as being a series of transition points by which parents help their children move toward independence. Children learn to walk, talk, and toilet themselves; they go to school, leave home, form their own partnerships, and take up careers. At each of these transition points the love a parent feels for each of his or her children may be subtly different, or may be expressed differently. Parents also experience joy through helping their children pass through these phases, although this joy may be experienced differently according to specific circumstances. Parents' pride and happiness in their child's increasing independence may be masked by a tinge of regret that they are "losing" their child.

Children with disabilities pass through a series of transition points in their lives, too, and although they may be very similar to those outlined above, they can also be radically different. Some children with disabilities will never be able to reach full independence, and this knowledge changes the nature of the parent-child relationship. The parent may feel that their duties and responsibilities will never end—that they will have a demanding child to care for forever. These fears can also become intertwined with worry about what will become of their child when they are too old to care for him or her any longer.

Raising a special-needs child may mean learning to find happiness in unexpected places, and to praise what others might find unremarkable. Your child's progress may be different or slow compared to that of other children, but it is important that you come to appreciate your child's achievements within the context of his or her ability.

It may also mean having to make some tough decisions at times: putting your child through a painful operation that will help him in the long run, removing her from a school she loves but that doesn't meet her needs, forcing him to attend physiotherapy sessions, enticing her to swallow a cocktail of vital medication every day.

Parents of children with disabilities know all about tough love. But they also know a lot about compassion, about patience, about doing their best under arduous circumstances. And, more than most, they are aware that a child's every achievement, every milestone is a moment to be savored and celebrated.

The Woman in the Mirror

Cheryl Veenstra

I SAW AN UNFAMILIAR FACE in the mirror today. She caught my eye as I rushed to start the day. I hardly recognized this woman. What had changed in her eyes? She was no longer young, naive, and viewing the world through rose-tinted glasses. What had caused the worry lines and thoughtful brow? How could she look so fragile and weary, yet also determined and strong?

Around some corner on the road of life she had been shaken to the core of her very being. There was a time when only tears and fears were reflected in those eyes. A doctor's unexpected words, the future suddenly uncertain . . . gray, shadowy images of the vague and scary concept of her child coming into the world "disabled." An incredible journey began that caught her by surprise and would take her places she never thought she would go. The journey had been long at times and she had shed tears of pain and tears of joy. She'd had hopes and dreams dashed in the blink of an eye. She'd asked the question Why?

She'd had friends fail her and not know what to say or how to help. She'd seen her child suffer. She'd cried silent tears into her pillow at night. Tears of exhaustion and fear, tears of helplessness and longing, tears of thankfulness and relief. Tears that are choked back during the day, but are unleashed like floodwaters in the safety of the night to wash away any walls being built up to protect her heart. Nights of worry blurring into days of endless responsibility. But then slowly but surely her broken heart begins to heal and mend.

The same pity she had once felt as she watched a mother hold her "special child" close was now looking back at her through the eyes of strangers. But a smile tugs at her lips as she suddenly real-izes that now she knows the secret! The hard-fought, carefully guarded, secret that was slowly revealed in the depths of her heart ... but only after the tears and anguish of the first days and weeks of this new life. The elusive truth that mothers of special children discover as they take their first faltering steps down this new path ... it was okay. She and her child could survive, even thrive! It was not as grueling and unforgiving a road as she had imagined. The fog, confusion, despair, and fear were slowly being replaced by peace, acceptance, contentment, joy, and gratitude. A mother's unique, unconditional love changes the equation that may look hopeless and tough to those outside looking in.

She will fight for, live for, and die for her child. These special children transform those around them into different people, stronger people. Dare I say it ... deeper people! Long gone are the days when all they had to worry about was where to vacation or what color minivan to buy. They now struggle with life-and-death medical issues. They must answer their child's questions about life's unfairness and pain. What remaining strength and energy they have is spent trying to make their family life as normal and happy as possible.

A twinkle returns to the eyes of the woman in the mirror as she takes a deep breath and remembers what she's been fighting for. How very worthwhile this journey has been! This child is an incredible gift and it is a privilege to be given the task of raising her. Her child is beautiful and perfect in her eyes. She longs for her child to be seen by the world through this filter of love, accept-ance, and potential. Could others take the time to see past this lit-tle girl's slower steps to see the life and love reflected in her eyes? Would her child be able to see herself through the filter of con-tentment that the woman has journeyed so long to discover?

Hope was rekindled as the woman's eyes grew brighter. The future remained uncertain, but the incredible, protective love she felt for her child threw a warm blanket over the cold, dark storm clouds that once threatened her very soul. As she threw open the doors of her heart, she felt the warm sun on her face and beheld a beautiful rainbow of intense beauty and unmistakable peace. Hope still comforts this woman who cries in the middle of the night. Love gets her through each day. Faith takes her hand and leads her around each corner and through each deep, dark valley. Peace soothes her heart as she relinquishes control of their destiny to One wiser and all knowing. Joy brings laughter and smiles to those tired eyes once again. Each day is recognized for the gift it is.

I gave that woman a smile as I left her at the mirror today. I'll see her again soon, and I'm curious to see how she will continue to change and grow. She's not the same young, carefree woman she used to be, but that is okay. I like who she is becoming and I feel comfortable in her life. The sun is shining, the day is brand-new, my child is humming, and God is so good!

He Makes Me Feel Very Proud

Maria Letizia

Not many people believe this, but I knew something was wrong with Cono before he was born. The doctor told me I was just tired, but I'd already had one healthy girl, and this time everything felt different.

When Cono was born, he was beautiful. He had the most beautiful little face, and still has. He looked perfect, but I knew he wasn't.

My mother had come from Italy two weeks before Cono was due and, as a result of complications and a mother's intuition, ended up staying six months. Just before she left, she turned to me and said, "Take him to the doctor. I think there is something wrong."

When Cono was twelve months old, the doctors told me he had brain damage. He would be severely retarded for the rest of his life. At the time my English wasn't very good and I didn't really understand what they were telling me.

I was only nineteen when I married, and twenty-four when I had Cono. I was a young girl who had never really had a life. And I never expected my life to turn out this way. After we got the diagnosis from the specialist, I lived like a zombie for months. I talked to people without listening and listened to people without really hearing what they were saying. Sometimes when Cono cried, I would have to make myself pick him up. Countless times I had to tell myself, "This is really my son, this is really happening to me."

Cono has very limited abilities because of damage to his frontal lobe. He has endured many painful operations to correct problems with his hips and spine. He had his first operation when he was only two weeks old and has had many since. We've just been told that his rib is fusing to his pelvis, which is causing him enormous pain. The doctor hopes that Cono can wear a brace rather than undergo another operation.

My son took his first steps when he was seven years old. I had promised my family I would take Cono to Italy for a visit when he could walk. Although I was excited about seeing everyone again, I was also very worried about how my relatives would react. I have a very big family in Italy. My brothers and sisters and cousins have lots of beautiful children. I wondered how they would react to Cono. As it turned out, I needn't have worried. My family loved Cono and everyone reacted to him well. It was weeks before some of my relatives even asked me questions about his condition. Cono and I went back to Italy again recently, even though all my friends said I was mad to take him on such a long journey. It was quite difficult, but it was worth it.

People haven't always treated Cono and me kindly. Once, when he was quite little, he went through a stage of being fascinated by watches. One day at the post office he went up to a man and started staring at his watch. The man was very rude to me, even though Cono was just a little boy.

I take pride in Cono's appearance and always dress him in lovely clothes. When we were in Italy, someone once said to me, "Why do you bother going to such an effort with his clothes?" I don't understand that sort of attitude. When people have problems like Cono, I think it is all the more important that they look as nice as possible. Disabled people are the same as you and me. They may have physical and mental difficulties, but we should treat them the same as we would anyone else, disabled or not.

Life has been really hard for everyone, especially my husband. He is a very reserved man, a very closed person. After the first year he never really spoke about Cono's condition again. I had friends I could confide in, and doctors and social workers I could talk to, but my husband had nobody. He has kept his feelings about Cono's disability to himself all these years.

One of the hardest things about raising Cono is that my elder daughter, Concetta, missed out on quite a lot because he took up so much of my time. She's a wonderful girl, and even though she's married now, she still comes to see Cono and me every day. There were many times when I couldn't take her to basketball practice or spend the time with her that I would have liked. Yet she has never complained and she loves her brother very much.

Cono didn't leave my side until he was sixteen years old. People had been telling me for a long time to get some respite care for him, but I hadn't listened. He was always a baby to me, and I didn't like the idea of handing my baby over to strangers, even for a short time. When I finally sent him to respite care, I came home and slept until one P.M. the next day. I hadn't realized how incredibly tired I was, how much of a burden I'd been carrying around all those years. Now he is in respite once or twice a month and I wish I had done it years ago.

Today Cono is twenty-two years old. He still cannot talk, and because of scoliosis he can only walk short distances. He is not toilet trained and can only eat finger food, such as sandwiches, unaided. He takes several medications to control mood swings and has developed a phobia about leaving the house. So we seldom go out these days, even on weekends.

I realized long ago that I can't live without him. When he's not here, even for a few hours, I feel completely lost.

I always think about the future and what will happen to Cono when I die, or when I am no longer able to look after him. I know that I can count on my daughter and her husband. Concetta has already said she and her husband will take care of Cono, but I am not sure about that. I don't want her to spend her life that way.

Despite everything, Cono is my whole life. I realized long ago that I can't live without him. When he's not here, even for a few hours, I feel completely lost. He needs me and I need him. He makes me feel very proud. Last year he wore a black suit and tie to his sister's wedding, and I thought he was the most beautiful boy I'd ever seen.

Holding Back the Tears

JUDY ASHBERG

I WAS A HAPPILY MARRIED WOMAN enjoying a thriving business career when I gave birth to my first child, a daughter named Sonia. As a result of birth trauma, Sonia developed cerebral palsy.

When Sonia was born, I was twenty-six years old, a young woman eager for both motherhood and career.

I always loved Sonia so much even though she could drive me crazy at times. Sonia is passionate and willful and, especially when she was younger, very moody. She has strong likes and dislikes, a wonderful sense of humor, and a great capacity to enjoy herself. She spends all her days in a wheelchair. Despite her limitations she is capable of manipulating those around her, and gets her own way most of the time. Her means of self-expression may be limited, but she has always been able to let everyone know just how she feels.

I always knew that I had not grieved sufficiently for what had happened to her and what had happened to me as her mother. I was a busy woman with three small children and a career. I made a promise to myself that one day I would give myself the time to have a really good cry, something much longer than my occasional bedtime outbursts.

When Sonia was six, I went to New York on business. My marriage was going through a difficult time and I felt very alone. As I sat in an impersonal hotel room in an unfamiliar city, I suddenly found myself crying—for my lost daughter, for the difficulty of being cheerful, for the effort required to be a "good mother" all the time, for the strain of putting on a brave face day after day, week after week, year after year. I cried because I had no one to share my burden with. I cried because I had been given so much but also because it was all so hard to bear.

I cried for three days. I did not know it was possible to cry so much, to stop crying for short periods and then find more and more tears running silently down my face. I did not know it was possible to have so many tears in one person. I wondered if I was having a nervous breakdown. Was this what it would feel like? I was a strong woman. I rarely cried. Surely this could not be happening to me.

Because I wanted to control my life and did not want people to think less of me, I had eschewed all forms of weakness. I learned that women's strengths and weaknesses are two sides of the same feeling. Weaker women find they can draw on the strengths of others to help themselves. Stronger women find it more difficult to acknowledge their vulnerability. All of us have both these qualities within. The weak envy the strong, and the part of me that had not previously owned up to it envied the weak. How much easier it is for vulnerable people to ask for help and support.

I did not have a breakdown, and the crying jag became a catalyst in my life. My marriage came to an end, and I lived as a single parent for three years. It was hard, but I managed. I had no choice, and it was preferable to being unhappy.

When Sonia was nine, she was offered a place in a residential home. I had put her name on the list and I believe she got priority because I was caring for her on my own. The organization, Norwood, is run by the most loving and caring people. For the staff that look after Sonia, nothing is too much trouble. I was not ready to let her go, but I knew that if I did not accept the offer, I might not have another chance when I did need it. I was capable of picking up the nine-year-old Sonia and carrying her upstairs or to the car, but I knew that was not going to be physically possible for me for much longer.

Sonia has lived at Norwood for many years now. I feel God looked after us all. Sonia was given what was best for her. Although she had a loving family, she used to find it difficult being with her brother and sister. She resented what they could do and she couldn't. At Norwood she is on a much more level playing field.

She is a competitive girl and can now compete on her own terms with the other residents.

The home is ninety minutes away by car, and I visit Sonia every month. When she was younger, she would come home for weekends. Now two people cannot lift her without a hoist, so it is no longer possible.

From an early age I had been brought up to have a career, and I have been fortunate to be successful in publishing. During all that time I never saw myself as a member of a caring profession, but much more as a strong, ambitious businesswoman. In my early forties, however, I began to work on a telephone crisis line. I discovered that I knew a lot about the pain of grief and loss and that there was a side of my personality that had real caring qualities. I trained as a bereavement counselor and am now qualified as a psychodynamic psychotherapist.

It was when studying to become a counselor that I had the opportunity to enter therapy for the first time in my life. Therapy allowed many years of pent-up emotions about Sonia to be released. I always thought I had coped well all these years—and in many ways I had—but therapy helped tremendously.

For so long I found it difficult to talk about Sonia for more than a few minutes without a lump coming into my throat. My voice would thicken and I would have to work hard to hold back tears.

If I had my time again, I would not change anything for myself, but I would have wished for an easier life for Sonia. But I do not really know about her inner world, and she cannot tell me. Maybe she has more peace of mind than I have. I will not know these answers in my lifetime.

Today I work both as a publisher and counselor. Sonia lives happily and I see her often. I love her so much. Although we have not lived together for many years, she is part of my being.

The next time I visit Sonia will be in a fortnight's time. We will celebrate her birthday. I will buy her some pretty girlie clothes and perfume and hand cream. I love massaging her hands and she loves having her nails painted. We will share some precious time together. She will be twenty-six.

When There Are No Words

Zan L. Liccione

Before Adrianna and Dante were born, or for that matter even thought of, a therapist once told my older two children and me that our family was "just too damn verbal!" It seemed like a joke at the time.

Alexa, now almost sixteen, began to speak at the tender age of eighteen months. She was a real talker, and by two and a half, when her brother Adam was born, she was speaking in full sentences and running circles around her peers. Adam was the same, speaking early and doing everything early. I know how to be a mom to "special" kids all right, but my kids were "special" in the other way—you know, the front end of the bell curve, like me. It seems so surreal sometimes when I think about the way things used to be. Having a grown-up-type conversation about the stars with a five-year-old can really skew one's perspective about normal kids.

Then Adrianna and Dante came along. Children of a different time of life, when mom is slower and plans are already laid. They are eleven months apart. They have a different father from Alexa and Adam. They seemed different from the start, but I thought it was because I was older. I thought maybe I was more stressed during these pregnancies. I thought that maybe I had simply forgotten what ordinary kids were like.

Throughout the days that seemed like years and the minutes that seemed like hours, I knew that something was not quite right. The hours on end of walking the floor, the months of having babies who did not like to be touched, the delays, the doctors, the questions, the aloneness with it all, and of course the vomit. Did I ever have a dress without vomit stains? Oh, that's right, it's not vomit; it's that polite word—what was it . . . oh, yes, *reflux*!

There was the news that Adrianna could not breast-feed since she could not keep my milk down. Swollen breasts, empty belly, what will work? How can this work? Will this be enough? There were to be admonitions to watch all the foods, be careful, check it all. There were never enough hands, or hours or dollars. How many villages did that First Lady say it took to raise a child? God, there were days when I wished I was in Africa, with a village all to myself! A village of hands and arms and feet to walk these crying children, to play with these tireless, relentless children, to feed them and wipe up and wash all the mess away.

So what does a mother say to those who stare at her when her babies scream because of clapping and cheers and anything louder than a sneeze? How does she explain that she forgot about the party, didn't make the cupcakes, doesn't have time for knitting or even thinking about yarn . . . odd, it seems like only yesterday that that little sweater only took me a month to make. Time . . . a luxury we forget, only to remember when there is no longer enough.

What is it like to be the mother of an angel or two? I am not sure. It seems to me that it is a special place, even without enough hands, or hours, or dollars. Even without enough love to go around and too tired to even get out of pajamas. To have two angels in the midst of the family, to know that even in a family that is too verbal there are two that may never speak a word.

It seems to me that it means learning another way to love. A way to love without saying a word or having a word said. It means letting go of intellect, of dreams, of wishes and things that seem to be the way things are—and loving in another way. Perhaps the other way is higher and demands more. Loving in the midst of the silence is difficult, but calls for change. It calls for change in oneself and in the world.

For me, living as a mother to two angels means seeing the angelic part in us all and seeing the smile for all its beauty. It means that even in the midst of a sleepless night with Fun Fruits stuck to my shoe, searching with desperation for the lost pacifier and all the things I do, it means loving. Simply that—loving. It means loving and knowing that I am loved. Some day I hope that will be enough.

Happiness Wears a Cheesy Grin

ROSE-MARY GOWER

W HEN YOU ADOPT a child with special needs, some people either doubt your sanity or think that you have suddenly sprouted a halo!

Our extended family was concerned that taking a child with a disability into our home would impact unfavorably on our three daughters. However, we felt that our family unit was one that could absorb and benefit from such a child. Naturally we discussed it with our girls and would not have gone ahead if they had been against the idea. They said, "Go for it!"

As a result my husband, David, and I took possession of a thirteen-month-old bundle of baby boy in April 1986. Any doubts soon melted away as John-Paul lost no time in finding a special place in all our hearts. Our own three daughters were sixteen, twelve, and ten at the time: they adored their little brother, and he fitted into our family immediately. The girls took pleasure in stimulating John-Paul, and by nineteen months old he was walking, which is quite early for a Down syndrome baby. John-Paul had been born in London, to young parents of Greek-Cypriot origin. The shock of having a Down syndrome baby was too much for them, and they immediately put him up for adoption. Fortunately John-Paul went to a loving short-term foster home.

As a young child, John-Paul had the quality of cuteness about him so beloved of little old ladies. I was astonished when we were out shopping one day and an elderly lady not of our acquaintance ran up to his stroller and kissed and hugged him! Her explanation was that he was so lovely and that "these children" like to be hugged and kissed! I don't think that she would be quite so enthusiastic if years later, as a hulking teenager, he were to return the compliment! Another thing that amazed me while John-Paul was growing up was the number of people who said, "You do dress him in a modern way, don't you?" I began to wonder whether people with Down syndrome were expected to wear a uniform proclaiming their disability.

When John-Paul was five years old, we moved to North Wales. Until then he had attended our local primary school in Cambridgeshire, England. Although his social life was good, we felt that John-Paul did not receive enough of the teacher's time—hardly surprising in a class of thirty-six children—and we decided to home-school him. Because John-Paul was a well-behaved child, this was not a hard decision to make: it would be good to have him at home all day. A special school was not an option we favored, as he might pick up undesirable behavior patterns.

The beauty of home schooling is that you can come up with innovative ideas, unbounded by the state-mandated curriculum. John-Paul's fine motor skills are not particularly well developed—he finds handwriting quite difficult—so I suggested that he write letters to celebrities in the hope of a reply. Like most children, he enjoys receiving mail, so this gave him an incentive to keep improving his writing skills. To date he has three scrapbooks full of letters ranging from the queen, several archbishops, the pope, and the chief rabbi to his favorite TV and pop stars.

John-Paul at seventeen, with his schooling behind him, is content to help us around the house and garden. He will never be able to live independently, but no matter, he is a pleasure to have around (which is more than can be said for some teenagers!). John-Paul's presence in our family has given us much joy. He has confounded the doubters who thought we were mad to adopt a child like him. Without exception, he is loved and respected by all who are fortunate enough to know him. People have been warmed by the big cheesy grin that lights up his face!

These are John-Paul's words: "I am happy, I love my family, life is cool."

The world would have been a poorer place if our son had not existed.

Outside of the Norm

Rich Tepper

Talking about life with my son often begs the question "Where should I begin?" Making sense out of the whole thing has been very difficult. Yet despite all of his disabilities, he has had a tremendous impact on me, and I have grown because of him.

My younger son is named Benjamin. He has many "special needs," but his syndrome is undiagnosed. When he was an infant, I think I was a somewhat emotionally detached dad. Looking back to when my older son, Matthew, was an infant, I think the same thing occurred. But as Matthew's ability to interact grew, so did my love for him. But I was confused with Benjamin. I saw how everyday, simple tasks and social interactions could be so challenging, and I wanted to help. But he didn't even look at me!! Would I ever be able to do the same things with Ben that I did with Matthew, would I experience the same joy? I would later learn the answer to be yes, but with a twist!

Benjamin is now turning three. I believe he knows that I'm "Dad" and, by realizing that, our bond has grown! All along I was waiting for Ben to learn the skills that are required for our interaction and growth. Really, it was I who needed to grow and mature. Ben's skills have been there from the beginning.

Ben is ever so special. And I am so in awe of his dedication and determination. I can't imagine how hard some of these things must be for him. Practically every single therapist or teacher who has ever worked with him has fallen in love with him. What father doesn't like to hear how adorable his son is? He tries so hard at therapy—stepping, climbing, reaching, pointing, and so on. He works so hard at his special instruction. He tries so hard to express what he wants. I love his determination! I could give him hugs all day. We play games now. I stack the blocks and he knocks them over and giggles. We build with Tinker Toys. I still help him insert the little pieces. We watch the movie *Toy Story* together, and even laugh at the same things. More recently, I have been involved in Ben's educational planning and school placement. The pride I felt when he was accepted to a special autism school could surpass that of anyone. I felt as though I had this glow on my face!

I love to talk about him, as you can probably tell by reading this. And I am very proud of who he is. For myself, learning to interact outside of the norm has been a challenge, but I am figuring it out. I love to play blocks with him and read him books. I love each and every time he reaches out for attention. Because of what I do, I sometimes get home around his bedtime. I head straight to his room so I can say good night, hoping he'll still be awake! I still face everyday challenges that to parents of a "typical" child may seem mundane. But if it brings joy to Benjamin, it's worth it! I can teach him things, but I hope he'll keep teaching me new things. Now it's time for the rest of the world to experience all that he has to offer!

A Gift of Lessons

KATHERINE KRISHNAN

SANTOSH IS MY FIRSTBORN. He is a soft-spoken, good-natured boy who loves to play outside and adores his younger sister. He also has cystic fibrosis (CF), a chronic, progressive, genetic disease. It affects many parts of the body, including the lungs as well as the digestive and reproductive systems. When he was diagnosed at nine months old, Santosh was not gaining weight or meeting milestones. With proper daily medication and care he is now a thriving four-year-old who attends preschool and enjoys life.

Instead of this disease being a disaster in my life, it has been a blessing to my marriage. My husband and I need each other's daily support to face our son's uncertain future. We realize that our children's health is more important than career, money, or anything else. I gave up an enjoyable legal career in order to care for Santosh, whose health was poor before his diagnosis. Although various people think I wasted an expensive education, my husband and I know better. While there are countless well-known joys associated with being a mother, I now appreciate the difficulties, such as sibling rivalry, temper tantrums, and a constant struggle for patience that face every at-home mother. I've also had to confront some of the challenges unique to mothers of children with major health issues. These include insurance battles, finding a good speech therapist, straightening out tangles at chronic-care pharmacies, rejection from my first-choice preschool, and explaining Santosh's medications to family members and babysitters. I've been with Santosh during blood draws, monthly vaccination shots for certain CF patients, a barium swallow, a CAT scan, and countless throat swabs, stool samples, and X-rays.

For all this I am grateful. Grateful that my son has a face he knows and loves by his side rather than a nanny's, and arms that can comfort him like no other. I'm thankful that he was given to us to care for, rather than being in a place or with people who are unable to provide him with the constant vigilance CF requires. We're indebted to diligent researchers for the therapies and medication that are available for CF patients. There is no cure yet, but there will be.

This disease has also made me love my daughter very dearly. Although she does not have CF, her chances of inheriting it were one in four. (I know of several families in which all the children have CF.) Leela is a miracle. I no longer take good health—hers or mine—for granted. I take better care of myself because I am the best caretaker for Santosh and Leela, and I would never want this important job to fall to someone else.

Cystic fibrosis has made me a more compassionate person. While waiting in a clinic at our CF center, I have seen children in all states of health, both mental and physical. I see the angst behind the hardened look on a parent's face when people look away from their disfigured or wheelchair-bound child, or the child with tubes running out of her nose. I see parents look at my son and wonder what he's doing there because he looks and acts normal. I empathize with them. I know that they did not expect to have a child in less than ideal health. Both my parents and my husband's parents had three healthy children, and our grandparents had only healthy children, too. We were shocked to be the couple in whose child a recessive, genetic disease surfaced.

Naturally there are moments when I am given to the scarier side of the disease. The life expectancy for people with cystic fibrosis is in the early thirties. I tear up nightly when I check on him, and say "thank you" for his silent breaths that are not overwhelmed by coughing. We have been lucky with his health thus far, and he has fared extremely well for a child of his age with CF. Yet I can become dismayed easily if I start reflecting on the challenges he has to face in his life—medication every time he puts food in his mouth, the fear of him contracting bacteria devastating to a CF patient's lung function, the fact that he may be infertile due to the disease, and even the difficulties of traveling to foreign countries in case of infection. Even the smaller questions can plague me: will children in school make fun of him due to frequent trips to the bathroom or his daily doses of medications? I pray not.

Fortunately those moments do not come as often as they used to. I am appreciative beyond imagination for his mental capacity and his ability to hug me and tell me that he loves me. I am focused on keeping Santosh nutritionally healthy and mentally strong. I want him always to have a positive attitude. I never want him to feel sorry for himself, because I don't. At least I try not to. He's lucky to have a disease that's manageable and, with the proper care, will allow him to do almost anything he wants to in life.

I often think that Santosh's life, including his CF, is a gift of lessons. I have learned that when faced with the possibility of your child's life being shortened, you hold him a little closer and imprint memories more firmly in your heart. I had taken so many things for granted before he came into my life. A healthy child was just one of them. CF did not fit into the expecta-

When faced with the possibility of your child's life being shortened, you hold him a little closer.

tions I had for the way my children's lives would be: that they would grow and talk normally, go to school, go to college, get married, and have children the way I did. Already those expectations have changed. Santosh did not speak sentences until he was over three years old, and he needed frequent speech therapy.

It took cystic fibrosis to teach me the lesson that life doesn't always go along with our wants or expectations. Life's difficult lessons can take over with gloom and doom—if you let them. Having this disease in our lives has paradoxically made it easier for me to accept the changes in the map I had for Santosh's life. I know now that the bottom line is that he's happy, healthy, and where he is supposed to be. He doesn't have to fit in to a world that I'd envisioned. He's himself. Perfect.

Spirituality

The possession of knowledge does not kill the sense of wonder and mystery. There is always more mystery.

ANAÏS NIN

Introduction

NEIL NICOLL

WHILE UNDERSTANDING an individual's spirituality is not usually an area that falls within the expertise of most psychologists, some of the parent stories collected in this book make it clear that a strong belief in a higher power can be of benefit to people grappling with a wide range of emotional issues.

A recent study published in *The Medical Journal of Australia* found strong links between an individual's religious conviction and their longevity. Not only did the spiritually aware apparently live longer, they were also healthier too, with lower blood pressure, cholesterol, and lower rates of certain cancers.

Similarly, the Center for the Study of Religion/Spirituality and Health at Duke University has conducted several studies that link godliness to reduced rates of suicide and depression and to higher rates of matrimonial bliss.

While this research is far from conclusive, it seems fair to suggest that having a strong religious conviction may make an individual more confident and trusting in life's outcomes, and therefore more able to cope with problems and crises as they arise.

I have called this chapter "Spirituality" rather than "Religion" because I have seen no evidence that it is only those who adhere to mainstream religions such as Hinduism, Islam, or Christianity who benefit from a faith in higher powers. The term *God* is used here simply for the sake of clarity; it does not imply that Christians and other monotheists are more likely to benefit from being true believers than people of different religious persuasions.

Lastly, the inclusion of this chapter does not suggest that religion is necessarily a component of successfully raising a child with disabilities. Spirituality is a very personal subject, and while some are highly dependent on their faith, others find no need for it at all. Both the agnostic and the devout can be equally fine parents.

The Role of Faith

We live in a complex, multicultural, multifaceted society where a diverse range of religions and moral beliefs, cultures, and traditions coexist. Yet, in secular societies such as those of Australia, the United Kingdom, and the United States, little thought or study has been devoted to understanding the impact of grief upon an individual's religious beliefs—the interface between faith and the grieving process, or the role that an individual's religious faith may play in supporting him or her through the grieving process.

Each of us experiences profound loss or grief in very different ways. People's reactions to such trauma are in part dependent upon their prior experience of life and its challenges, upon personality and temperament, the depth of available support networks, social and economic circumstances, and so on. It is hardly surprising, therefore, that religious beliefs can have a profound influence on the ability to cope with the birth of a disabled child.

A Test of Faith

Those who see their faith as some kind of protection against harm may find the arrival of a special-needs child a doubly shattering experience. It is not uncommon for those with normally strong religious beliefs to become deeply conflicted following a trauma, as they struggle to reconcile their role as a "good" person with what may seem like a "punishment" bestowed on their family by a higher power. The fact that "bad" things can happen to "good" people is not necessarily easily accepted, and some families may need considerable support to help them understand that a special-needs child is nobody's fault.

Indeed, some belief systems actually enshrine the concept of direct retribution for sin. To followers of such religions, it may appear that a disabled child is "payback" for past misbehaviors, perhaps even some indiscretions that may have occurred in a past life.

In extreme cases, previously faithful people may even begin questioning the existence of a higher power. In his seminal work *When Bad Things Happen to Good People,* Rabbi Harold S. Kushner offers a partial solution to the "Why me?" questions from a Judeo-Christian viewpoint. He suggests that perhaps God may choose not to control everything, a decision that effectively renders the world imperfect. And in an imperfect world, unpleasant and stressful occurrences should be expected.

Reaffirming Your Beliefs

While trauma sends some people off to question their faith, others cling to theirs all the more firmly, aware that it offers them strength and the extra hope they require to carry on. While there is little empirical research into the role a strong faith may play in the birth of a disabled child, common sense suggests

While trauma sends some people off to question their faith, others cling to theirs all the more firmly.

that a person who feels strong and confident and believes that such a life crisis has a greater purpose has an upper hand when it comes to coping with grief.

Religious commitment offers believers more than strength of purpose; it can also be a guiding hand in terms of uncertainty, a path to follow when difficult decisions need to be made. Spirituality offers a safety net of sorts—a place where your troubles and doubts can be set aside in favor of the belief that either a solution can be found (and you are not alone in seeking it) or that your child's situation serves a greater good.

Religious certainty can also be used by parents as an explanation for any positive outcomes that occur with their child. A parent may see progress in their child as a confirmation that they have been helped by God or another higher power to make the right decisions. Their disabled child is proof to them of God's purpose and a challenge to them as parents. Appreciating that their special-needs child is a gift and being able to celebrate their successes and overcome their challenges is seen as proof of God's faith in them as parents.

Something Much Bigger Than All of Us

Claudia Enright

I GREW UP IN AN ALCOHOLIC FAMILY, where my emotional needs were never met. As a consequence I have struggled my whole life with relationships and have always felt that if only I had more money or looked a certain way or said the right things, then perhaps I would be better at forming friendships.

I started drinking at a very early age and learned quickly to cling on to whatever I could to maintain my sanity. In my mid-twenties, after years of emotional hell, I finally sought help and slowly started regaining my life. I met a good man, married, and became pregnant with my first child.

Although I loathed being pregnant, I instantly loved my newborn daughter, Monica. The day she was born I cradled her in my arms and felt certain that, finally, my life was back on track, this time for good.

Three days later, however, everything changed. Monica cried constantly day and night. Sleep deprived and anxious, I'll admit there were days when I felt I hated my newborn daughter. "Get this kid away from me," I thought. "What did I do to deserve this?"

I went into therapy for postnatal depression and began to pray to God every day, begging him to give both Monica and me a little peace.

Finally, at around three months of age and after countless ear infections, formula changes, and doctor's visits, Monica's constant screaming began to settle down. Relieved that I had managed to get through those months without killing my daughter, I thanked God and began to look forward to better times.

Once again, however, I was to be disappointed. When Monica's crying slowed down, so did her growth. Soon every doctor's visit was a series of endless questions about weight and what we were feeding her. Before long I was questioning my ability as a mother all over again. As Monica's weight continued to drop despite all my best efforts, I found that family members were looking at me as the culprit, somehow using Monica's failure to thrive as evidence that my wild past was still not fully behind me.

I exhausted myself trying to prove my worthiness. I became obsessed with Monica's weight, and visited an endless round of doctors, none of whom could explain her condition.

In the midst of all this my husband lost his job and we moved to Kansas City. For the next two years the children's hospital there prodded and poked and filled my baby with growth hormones until, finally, they were able to diagnose her with a rare condition known as Floating-Harbor syndrome.

From the moment I received that diagnosis, I became my daughter's advocate. Realizing that she had become a guinea pig for the doctors to try various medications out on, I insisted she be taken off some of her treatments, and I turned instead to a holistic doctor, who recommended a radical change in diet.

Before long, Monica was sleeping soundly and was much more settled in her behavior. I realized then that I did know what was best for my daughter and that I could make a difference in her life. I started listening to my gut instead of what other people told me was best.

I decided to be strong and to never give up on Monica. This wasn't always easy to do. At times, when doctors were putting tubes in her head, I would cry and ask God why he made her suffer like this. At other times, I would resent my life and I would hate the fact that I had given up my freedom for this demanding little girl.

One day I drew up an inventory of all the countless hours I

spent each day caring for my daughter. I realized that nobody had ever spent that much time on me growing up, and I felt old emotions and old grudges resurface.

My husband traveled for his work, so I was often left to care for Monica on my own. There were days when I would have been happy merely to have a shower in peace. Although Monica is four and a half, she has a mental age of two, and even now will scream if I leave her alone for even a brief period of time.

After one particularly bad day I found myself venting my anger on God again, demanding to know why I was being punished in this way. Suddenly I realized that Monica was God's gift to me, not my sentence. God had given me Monica because he loved me and because he wanted me, after all my early unhappiness, to really know what love meant.

Love, he was teaching me, didn't necessarily have to be perfect or pure or easy. It was okay to get angry with myself and my daughter sometimes; it was okay to feel frustrated and misunderstood. It was okay to sometimes not want to take care of my daughter. Beneath it all, I loved her very much, and that was what was important.

All my life I had felt unworthy of love, and had spent Monica's early years trying to prove myself capable of being a good mother, trying to show the world that I was good enough after all. Now God was showing me that it didn't matter what others thought— he thought I was good enough. My child had imperfections, it was true, but all of us are imperfect in some way or another.

Through Monica, God showed me that living in this world isn't about me, it's about others and what I can do for them. I'm not walking around with a halo these days, by any means, but I do walk around happy in the knowledge that I am loved by something much bigger than all of us.

Monica and I still have a long way to go. For others like us, I would say express all your feelings, be honest in your emotions, even if what you are feeling makes you uncomfortable sometimes. Know that this journey you are on is a powerful one that will either make or break you. If you succeed, the end result can be enlightenment.

I am truly blessed to have been chosen to be the mother of Monica Grace. After all my struggles I can honestly say I know love.

The Making of an Honest Woman

Natalie Hale

BEFORE MY SON, Jonathan, was born, I thought I was an honest woman. A good citizen, the kind of person who'd return the money if a cashier gave her too much change.

But when Jonathan entered my life, he caused a paradigm shift I can only liken to a cosmic quake off the planetary charts. The baby in my arms stripped away all pretense, all dishonesty. No one would ever be able to look at my child and pretend that he was "normal." Living with that reality, I soon found that Jonathan's disability stripped the veneer off all my life's pretenses.

As I began to live with this truth, I saw that much of my behavior had been dishonest. I had laughed when I wanted to cry, was superficially friendly to people who repelled me, and wasted precious time on useless pursuits.

Now I loved and lived with a child who, as a friend said, "goes straight to the store." My friend meant that kids like Jonathan have neither the heart nor the capability for dishonesty or pretense. They cut through the red tape of life and go directly to Truth. I am convinced that we cannot be parents of children like this without belonging to the same visionary club as they do. Our understanding is forever expanded, forever altered. There is no way back to unawareness.

As the primary caretaker of the disabled child cradled in my arms, I soon realized that in order to help him, I had to get on his vibrational level and learn to see with his eyes. Attuning to my child, I began to see that even as an infant he could see and sense things I could not. I observed and tried to learn.

For example, I noticed that when Jon and I were in the company of someone who saw his disability rather than his potential, he gave them what they expected. He slumped over his stroller, tongue hanging out, eyes glazed over. When we were with friends who saw past his exterior "cosmic disguise," Jon's eyes were bright and eager, he sat tall, and handed out his best smiles and laughter. These friends, too, got what they expected.

I soon realized the wisdom of noting Jon's judgments about other people. If Jon was his best self with a stranger, it was a safe bet that the stranger was a good soul; if Jon drooled, I took the cue to stay clear of that person. Ritualistic social events that I had formerly valued now became meaningless, and I avoided them. Conversely, time spent with friends who really understood me and valued my child became more precious.

But most important was the change in my inner vision. From infancy my son seemed to be able to see or sense things that my eyes and senses were blind to. Gradually, over the years, I learned to be more aware of that other dimension, that realm he seemed to see so effortlessly. He has taught me subtly and well over the last eighteen years.

One day when Jon was two years old, I tucked him into his seat in the back of my car, directly behind my seat. The back of my seat was high, and there was no way for him to see me. I got into the car and reached for the ignition. As was my habit, I paused for a minute, closed my eyes, and mentally prayed for our safety. When I opened my eyes and turned the key, Jon said aloud from the back seat, "Amen!"

Then there was the day I found myself in a bad mood. I was determined not to let on to Jon, and covered it up with cheerfulness. I succeeded, or so I thought. As I served Jon his lunch in the dining room, I said brightly, "Don't forget to say your own grace, kiddo." Then I went into the kitchen, where I heard him pray out loud, "And please help Mama not-be-bad-mood."

So much for even subtle dishonesty! I realized I could never fool him; he could see into my soul from the next room. I had to be real. Whatever I was, I had to be honest about it. And after being honest about what was going on within me, I then had the option of changing. Not always an easy task.

Having a child with special needs and being taught Truth by that child is spiritual boot camp. It is open-heart surgery for those who are ripe for such a transformation. We have probably all heard it said that parents of disabled children are carefully chosen in the spiritual realm, and that what we are asked to experience is thoughtfully designed in advance. I be-

Having a child with special needs and being taught Truth by that child is spiritual boot camp.

lieve beyond doubt that this is true, and that there are no cosmic accidents.

I believe that we agree to parent these little souls in advance of our arrival here. We agree to teach them and to be taught by them. Being the parent of a child with special needs propels us into a finer realm of truth, one where life must be lived differently, in awareness of that truth. Truth in this case embraces not only honesty but also awareness, patience, endurance, creativity, wonder, and anything else we've signed up to learn. And as our children's disabilities are ongoing, we are effectively not permitted to slip back, ever, into a life of "not truth."

As a formerly less-than-honest woman, I much prefer the realm into which I've been propelled. It's not always easy, but if I ever forget that I signed up for this training, I can trust with certainty that, in some way, Jonathan will remind me.

Butterfly Wings

MICHELLE CHRZCZONOWICZ

I CONSIDER MYSELF a caterpillar in a cocoon before my daughter, Matisse, was born, and I hope that I am gradually growing into a butterfly with brilliant colors on my wings and being a mother that Matisse would be proud of. I have learned so much from my little one and can't imagine how I ever considered my life to be fulfilling before she came along.

Matisse was born at thirty-four weeks by an emergency Caesarean. We had noticed her movements had decreased to zero within twenty-four hours, and during a visit to the hospital the monitor showed her to be in fetal distress. My obstetrician discovered, when he delivered her, that the umbilical cord was tightly wrapped around her leg five times and loosely around her neck once. Another twenty-four hours and she would have been delivered as a stillborn.

Her diagnosis was lack of oxygen resulting in severe cerebral palsy and secondary microcephaly. My husband, Matthew, and I were sat down in a room that we later came to refer to as "the much-feared and -loathed bad-news room" and were told not to expect her to survive the next forty-eight hours. The neonatologist predicted that her brain injury was so severe that her organs would slowly shut down and she would die. Of course this was devastating to be told, and we held each other and cried and cried and cried. All the while I kept thinking everyone was playing a joke and would soon start laughing and telling me that all would be perfect for my little girl. Part of me is still waiting for that unattainable miracle.

Meanwhile the practical side of me took over, and we asked

the specialists to get a priest to come in and baptize Matisse immediately. It is a funny thing how in times of trauma you suddenly find comfort in your faith, whether it be religion or spiritual beliefs. Matt and I had both been raised Catholics. I felt my religion was forced down my throat and hence was no longer a "practicing" Catholic. Over the last few years we had decided to have a naming ceremony for our kids rather than the specific rites of passage performed by the Catholic Church. Yet suddenly we felt the strong need to baptize our little one and hope that God would keep her safe.

Matisse stayed in the neonatal intensive care unit (NICU) for three weeks, getting a little stronger each day, although every sign of progress we saw was quashed immediately and given a clinical reason by the doctors caring for her. It was very frustrating being told your daughter's movements are reflex only and not a true sign of progress. We were told not to expect much from her at all for the very few days they expected her to live. How I would love to take her back to the doctors now and pull a childish face saying "Ner, ner, ne, ner ner!"

Matisse came home at thirty-seven weeks. The reason she was allowed to come home early was simply because there was nothing more the NICU could do for her, and we were adamant that we were not going to let her die in that wretched hospital. Matt and I had just bought our first home and moved in two days before we brought Matisse home with us, so it was very important to us that she should die in her own bed in her family home.

We were taught how to tube-feed her, suction her (as she had no swallowing reflex), and all the while the doctors, never the nurses, would reinforce just how dire the situation was. They drummed into us that she would never swallow, eat, move, see, or hear. We tried to be realistic and listen to them; however, a part of us had no intention of giving up on our sweet little angel, and we believed she would improve.

We made a deal with God, pleading that if he could give us time with Matisse, we would be happy with whatever package she came in, no matter how severely affected she would be. In return we would be forever grateful for whatever time we had with her and would understand when he decided it was time to take her.

We made a deal with God, pleading that if he could give us time with Matisse, we would be happy with whatever package she came in.

Well, so far he has answered our prayers. Of course I am human and naturally selfish, especially when it involves my husband and daughter. I have had Matisse with me for almost a year now, and I have absolutely no intention of letting her go. She has developed her own little personality and, for all the crap she has been subjected to, she is still a happy little girl.

One thing I remember saying when Matisse was still in the NICU was that I would be more than happy if all she could ever do was smile, giggle, and know who Matt and I were. My dream came true when Matisse was eight months old: she gave us a smile and a belly laugh that totally rocked my world. And what made it even better was the fact that it came in response to us—we had been tickling her and making funny noises when her whole face lit up. It was truly the most magical experience and one I will never, never forget. We are now graced with her small squeals of delight so often, yet we still never take a single snort, giggle, or smile for granted.

Since Matisse we have certainly changed our attitudes and views on life in general. Suddenly we give a damn about stem cell research, alternative therapies, and so on. We no longer concern ourselves with the trivial issues in life, such as arguing with the driver of the car that just took our parking space, nor are we ever torn, the way I was just the day before Matisse was born, over what colors and sizes of clothes to buy for our child.

We appreciate life, and we appreciate our beautiful, happy little baby. Okay, so she may never walk or talk, but there is no reason why we can't try to teach her or find other ways to help her become mobile and learn to communicate with us. We also appreciate the friends we have made as a result of all the different therapies we are trying for Matisse, people with whom we have formed an instant bond on account of our special-needs kids.

I look back over the last year, and yes, it has been an incredibly tough road; however, we have also been very fortunate along the way. The day Matisse was delivered, my obstetrician also shared another surprise with us by telling me that I have only one ovary and that my uterus was only half formed. He was surprised that we'd even been able to get pregnant. Four months later and I was back in his office, pregnant again. Our second little one is due in six weeks, and it will be another daunting experience since this time we will have to learn how to care for a "typical" baby. Positive thinking is simply amazing.

Recently Matt and I were watching a video of Matisse when she was in the NICU. She had looked so tiny and helpless connected to all these machines that we could never take our eyes off her for fear something bad would happen. It brought up so many buried emotions—we had really forgotten what a hard time we had had. Many friends, relatives, and medical professionals have commented on how strong and together we were. I never understood why they admired us since I couldn't imagine dealing with our situation any other way.

Now that I look back, we could quite easily have given up and trusted what the doctors were telling us; we could have fallen to pieces and felt sorry for ourselves. I realize that Matt and I were keeping each other strong during that time. We stuck it out together, talked, and weren't afraid to cry in front of each other or to share our fears. Above all, we made a pact to fight for Matisse and only let her go when she gave us a sign. We allowed ourselves to grieve the loss of the baby we were expecting, yet that didn't mean we were ungrateful for the baby we were given. I sincerely believe that Matisse chose us, that she is here for a reason, and that together we will do our very best to help her fulfill her purpose. As a close friend said to her eight-year-old daughter, "Matisse is here for such an important purpose that she doesn't even need to know how to walk or talk in order to achieve it."

I love the person I have grown into and I feel like I have been welcomed into a very special group of people who all share this secret bond: we love life and can honestly say we wouldn't want our lives any other way now that we have our special children. I have grown my butterfly wings; they still have a long way to go before all the beautiful colors come through, but that is half the fun of living.

She's Worthy of a Dream Come True

TONY PHILLIPS

SOME DREAMS SEEM SO REAL, they scare us. Others take us into fantasy worlds we know could never exist.

This dream I need to share leaves me hoping that dreams can come true. In my dream I had fallen asleep in a reclining chair. I was awakened from a fitful slumber by a presence at the foot of my chair. I would later learn I was still dreaming, a dream within a dream, if you will. The chair's leg rest suddenly jerked under my feet. I opened my eyes to find my precious daughter standing there proudly seeking acknowledgment. She was smiling and giggling while yanking back and forth on the chair. Her head was swaying to and fro as she struggled to apply her weight to her efforts.

I jumped from the chair and snatched her up into my arms, pulling her close to my chest. I was overcome with the purest sensation of joy. I hugged her close as we laughed and cried together. Glancing across the room, I could see the open door to her room and, beyond that, her bed with the blankets dragged off onto the floor. Scooping up the blankets, I lowered her into the bed, where she immediately began thrashing her body from side to side.

"It's okay, Cami, you need to go back to sleep now," I whispered. It was then that I realized her nightclothes were soaked with perspiration, as were the sheets under her body.

The unexpected sensation must have caused me to awaken (this time for real), because I suddenly found myself sitting upright in bed. The very first thing I felt was anger. I was mad about ending the dream I didn't want to leave. I felt foolish falling for the false images. I was mad at God for the fact that I had to resort to dreaming for the experience of something so simple. I was sad that the dream might never come true. Our daughter has cerebral palsy, epilepsy, and is legally blind. The sum of her disabilities makes any hope of ever seeing my dream come true quite remote. The next morning I found peace with God and with the dream. I enjoy it now for the pleasure it brought, if only for the shortest time. The only thing I want to take from the dream is the purest sense of joy and happiness I think one could ever experience. The emotions I felt came from another plane, a different level of awareness. Maybe the source was God. I'd like to think so. It felt more intense than the most powerful of drugs. It gave me a feeling I don't think I'll ever duplicate, not in this world anyway.

The dream gives me hope. Hope for answers and medical advances. Hope for a miracle from Jesus in answer to prayers made for healing. The child is worthy of a better chance. Born to a minor and adopted at birth, she has all the love and the best medical treatment anyone could offer. She travels regularly to specialists in two different distant cities. She puts up with two or three different medications three times a day. She wears special braces on her legs and one arm to stabilize and stretch her limbs. She stands and sits only with the assistance of apparatuses complete with lots of belts and buckles. She endures twice-daily sessions of stretching and exercising, along with up to four visits each week to therapists for physical, occupational, and speech workouts.

She works hard, along with her mother, to attain even the smallest of gains. Her rigid body, plagued by continuous spasms, and her brain that lacks coordination between the left and right halves make mobility nearly impossible. Her ability to sit up unassisted or to grasp objects with her one good arm have been milestones to date. Anyone can see all the pain and frustration our little angel endures each day as she battles her own body. She fights through muscles racked in spastic contractions, she focuses hard to overcome a brain without the ability to control balance and to coordinate movements. She squints through the one eye capable of limited sight from a narrow range of something akin to tunnel vision. She awakens in the middle of the night, most likely from the muscular cramps. While awake, she thrashes her limbs and body while singing happy songs of gibberish.

Yet, throughout it all, each day she remains a bundle of sunshine. The girl refuses to quit. She finds creative ways to do things others take for granted. She likes playing with a baby doll, using her one good arm, the "club" arm, and her mouth or chin to wrap it up or give it a bottle. She takes great pride in her independence, however small it might be. Count on one thing from this little girl: she seldom gives up her positive spirit and cheery expressions of love.

She shares her sunshine with everyone she meets. Forever displaying her endless smile to friends and strangers alike. I've heard people say "dreams can come true" and "if you want it bad enough, anything is possible." If dreams could be judged and granted on some scale of worthiness, I know I'll see this one come true. Believing a major advance like I witnessed in "the dream" possibly will keep our faith and hope alive. Can you imagine? A beautiful little girl with the ability to walk over and wake up her daddy. If anyone reading this knows how to control dreams so that one can relive them, please let me know. I have one I'd like to repeat, over and over again.

To Love and Be Loved

KIMBERLY NAVA

When I was pregnant with our first child, people would ask if we wanted a boy or a girl. I'd reply that my husband wanted a boy and I wanted a girl, but really we just wanted our baby to be healthy. I knew about those poor souls who had the burden of a disabled child, and I felt sorry for them. Through an ultrasound, we learned we were having a girl, and we looked forward to our beautiful, healthy child and all the potential her future held for her.

We named her Celeste, which means "heavenly."

As she got older, and her peers talked more and more, she was obviously behind in speech. I'd take her to doctors, and they told me to wait and see—"She'll catch up." My dad and my husband told me I was making a big deal out of nothing, that Einstein didn't talk until he was five, and that she'd catch up.

We did have her assessed, and she began receiving speech therapy for a severe speech delay. One day the director of preschool speech therapy told me that Celeste was not understanding some things they would expect a child her age to understand. Since she was my first, I didn't know what she should understand or what was typical. I asked her to tell me the truth, did she think it was because she was not getting enough stimulation at home. She said, no, she believed it was neurological.

I didn't believe her. I assumed it was my fault. So now I was really beating myself up, feeling guilty, but also reading everything I could get my hands on about speech delays and language development.

That summer Celeste had her first seizure, stopped breathing, and turned blue. I had never seen a seizure before and didn't know what was happening. I was hysterical, so my husband came and calmly took our daughter and held her. I was screaming on the phone to the 911 operator, who was trying to calm me down. I thought I was watching my child die before my eyes, and I was completely unable to help her.

Celeste started preschool at Head Start the next autumn. As I watched her interact with the other kids, she seemed vulnerable. Some of the kids protected her, took care of her, and helped her, whereas others teased her like they might a younger child. I was starting to see that she was different to her peers.

Although I didn't admit it to myself at the time, I had always placed a higher value on people who were more intelligent. When it became obvious that my daughter would not be as intelligent as her peers, I really had to rethink my values. I had always believed and paid lip service to the idea that all people have rights, including the disabled. But I still elevated intelligence, and that had been my primary hope for my child. But when I thought about my beautiful daughter's learning difficulties, I refused to believe she did not have the same worth as any other child. I could not accept that.

When it became obvious that my daughter would not be as intelligent as her peers, I really had to rethink my values.

She may never be a rocket scientist, I thought, but she has every bit as much inherent value as any other child. Still, I asked myself repeatedly, what is it that gives us our inherent human value? If it's not our intelligence, then what is it?

Finally, after much soul searching, I decided that our value comes from our spirits; it is our ability to love and be loved. I came to see our bodies as a home that holds our spirits and that, regardless of whatever part of the home may not be working properly, there is still a spirit residing there that can love and be loved.

I came to believe that God is love.

My daughter reveals the glory of God and, because of her, I

have learned one of the most important spiritual lessons. It is the absolute, unconditional love of God, the Universe, and Spirit. The most important thing anyone could ask for.

When our daughter was assessed again at age six, I was still shocked to learn that she is mildly retarded. I had no idea. However, after taking some time to think it through, everything made sense. All the forgetfulness that I assumed was "accidentally on purpose" and that I mistook for stubbornness was probably occurring because she actually did not understand an instruction.

The hardest thing, through all of this, was dealing with the criticism of other people, and my own self-criticism. It stung when a neighbor, whose children I baby-sat, said, "If I had her for a week, she'd be talking." I gave my family videos to watch and brochures to read about epilepsy, which to this day have not been looked at, but that did not stop anyone from offering an opinion and commenting about whether I am doing enough or working hard enough to find a "cure" for her epilepsy.

I am her primary caretaker. I am the one who has had to live twenty-four hours a day, seven days a week, 365 days a year, with my daughter's behavior problems and hypersensitivity. I am the one who held her and comforted her during and after her seizures when she was a preschooler, while simultaneously juggling the demands of a toddler and a newborn. I am the one who has had to stand by and watch helplessly when other kids treat her cruelly, which feels to me like they are sticking daggers through my heart. No one has worked harder on her behalf than I have.

One thing that I have learned is that blaming me is part of my family's denial—and my own. If it is my fault that she is not speaking, or learning, or behaving, then I don't have to acknowledge her disabilities. We can all pretend that there is nothing wrong with her, that she is not retarded, that she's not overly sensitive. It's easier for me to believe that it's me, it's my fault.

The second hardest thing has been navigating the school system. I entered the system naively assuming there would finally be people there, experts, who understood my daughter's disability, who understood the incredible stress parents are under. We have received some great help from some wonderful people within the school system, but the system itself, in my experience, is dehumanizing. We came seeking help, relief, and understanding, and instead it sometimes feels as though, because our children consume a larger share of resources than the regular-education kids do, we are the enemy of the school system.

What's interesting is that when I look back on all of this, I realize that the most important thing I have learned is not how to negotiate bureaucratic red tape. It is not what I have taught myself about the brain and neurological functioning. It is not what I have discovered about human behavior and the ways people can be subtly or overtly cruel or well-meaning but ignorant.

I have realized that it's okay to complain, and it is okay to talk about how I really feel. Sometimes people are shocked when I talk honestly about my negative feelings and frustrations about my disabled child. It's almost as if, because her disabilities are not her fault, I have no right to feel frustrated, exasperated, and exhausted. Yet to do anything else is to be fake. Now, however, I've also learned whom to complain to, because not everybody is equipped to deal with my reality.

Above all, the most important thing I have learned since having a disabled child is that God is love, that we are all loved, and that the whole purpose of our existence is to love and be loved.

Laughter

Laughter is higher than all pain.

ELBERT HUBBARD

Introduction

Neil Nicoll

A MOTHER WAS OUT walking with her daughter, a twelve-year-old with Down syndrome. They happened to meet a female acquaintance in the street and stopped to chat. The girl, who had never met the woman before, gazed at her solemnly and in a serious tone said, "You are very, very old."

Most parents would be horrified to find themselves in this situation. This particular mother, however, quietly apologized to the woman, reminded her daughter that honesty is not always necessarily the best policy, and a little later, when she was alone, burst out laughing.

After years of worrying about her daughter's penchant for speaking the brutal truth, this mother had finally come to accept the lighter side of life with her daughter. After all, her daughter didn't speak out of malice or a desire to be cruel. She was a kind-hearted girl who simply "told it like it was" and didn't understand normal social conventions. It was, she had learned, okay to laugh.

Laughing Is Allowed

Children do funny things. Sometimes their humor is intentional, often it is not. As every parent knows only too well, not only are a child's antics often amusing but grown-ups can do and say some pretty silly things as well. Attempting to cope with the many trials of raising children can be the source of a great many amusing situations, especially on those occasions when things don't quite go as planned.

Laughter is the most natural of cathartic processes, and its occurrence tends to reflect a sense of well-being in times of stress, our ability to separate ourselves from stressful events and appreciate the irony and humor of situations.

The fact that your child is disabled doesn't mean you're not allowed to find them funny as well. While outsiders might look at your child and feel saddened by his disability, as a parent you see the real person in his entirety.

Of course it is necessary to discriminate between laughing with and laughing at someone, and laughter should never be cruel or sarcastic when children are involved. Nor should they ever be the object of ridicule. However, laughter is very important for parents coping with the demands created by disability, as a means of catharsis and as a means of separating from situations that can be very fraught.

The Benefits of Laughter

Everyone feels better after a good, long belly laugh. Now science has discovered what everyone suspected all along: laughing is good for both our physical and our psychological health.

Laughter reduces stress. Researchers at Loma Linda University in California found that immune function was enhanced and stress hormones reduced in subjects who viewed humorous videos. When people are stressed, they produce a hormone called cortisol; laughter lowers cortisol levels and returns the body to a more relaxed state.

Laughter reduces minor pain too. When we chuckle, our bodies produce painkilling hormones called endorphins.

Laughter enables parents to experience the sadder and more difficult aspects of parenting in a less direct manner. Laughter releases pent-up emotion in a socially acceptable way and allows parents to share their difficult experiences with others in a less confrontative manner. Laughter enables parents to see, perhaps for the first time, the funny side of their lives. Laughter enables others to share and understand the lives of parents with disabled children.

Another important function of laughter is to express delight and happiness, and children with disabilities afford parents many opportunities to experience these emotions. New skills are learned, challenges overcome, and sudden progress made. These are all reasons to feel happy, and laughter is the natural response. Under these circumstances, laughter is a measure of the degree to which parents have come to terms with their child's disability and the extent to which they have accepted the reality of their situation.

I'm in the Army Now

Ellen Forrest

I ONCE THOUGHT I knew what life was about. At twenty-nine I was happily married with a two-year-old child and another on the way. My future was in place, and I knew my place in it. Then my world turned upside down. I met my daughter.

I had been drafted into an army I didn't know existed. Basic training involved insecurity and uncertainty, and learning terms like *neurologist, respite, case manager, funding sources,* and *infant stimulation.* It meant slowly accepting that our beautiful, perfect daughter had physical disabilities and was going to lead us on a different path than the one we had imagined. That she would lead us to be different people than we had imagined, learning a new way to see the world, learning to find the humor in almost everything.

When Kate was two, I went numb. Literally. My daughter had misunderstood the parent manual that states that all newborn babies sleep twenty out of twenty-four hours. Kate slept four out of twenty-four on a good day. I was so far past exhaustion, I couldn't feel. I was in shock. I tried to understand that my daughter might never walk, talk, or function in any productive way, but I couldn't. Although I loved her desperately, I felt I'd given birth to the wrong baby. The baby I'd been carrying was healthy with a bright, active future. This baby was sick, unable to eat enough to gain weight, cried constantly, had no future that I could recognize, and I didn't know how to be her mother. So I went numb.

When Kate was four, I despaired. I cried all the time. Little girls all around us were going off to ballet classes and playing in the park. My daughter was still trying to hold her head up. She was beautiful with an incredible smile. She was happy all the time. But I couldn't see that. I pitied her. The thought of how hard her life was going to be was tearing me apart. We were at the park one day watching the kids play. I was crying, as usual, thinking about how my poor little baby would never be able to do what the other kids were doing. No slides, no swings, no jump rope. Then I looked down at her. She wasn't crying. She was laughing. Kate was watching the same kids I was and she was laughing! It hit me then that she was okay with having this disability. It was simply part of her life and she was coping just fine. It was me who couldn't be with it. She was much happier than I was, so who did I really pity?

After that my crying jags had more to do with me than with her. I cried for the mother I wanted to be and used to be. The mother of normal, healthy children, who didn't have to have therapists and doctors and all kinds of strangers involved in her life. A mother who knew how to meet her child's needs, a mother who could look forward to her daughter's first date, first kiss, first dance, to her daughter's wedding and to being a grandmother. I wanted to accept her as she was and stop wanting more, but I couldn't do it.

When Kate was six, I was sitting on the floor and Kate was lying on a mat beside me. I was sobbing and crying out loud, "I can't do this anymore, someone needs to take this from me." I had never been a particularly spiritual person, but at that moment I felt an indescribable sensation and understood that my request had been answered. My tears dried up instantly. I felt at peace. I knew that the future might not be what I'd planned but that there was a different plan in place. I was doing what I was supposed to do. I was doing okay as a mom. I wasn't supposed to know everything, I was just supposed to do the best I could. I understood all this in a split second. It was weird and wonderful and I can still feel it like it was yesterday.

When Kate was ten, I discovered I was tired of worrying, tired of feeling bad, and tired of crying over every disappointment. I was thirty-nine years old and I was tired of myself. It was time for a change. I didn't go to a self-help seminar, or read any books on the subject. I didn't get counseling and I didn't join a yoga class. I learned to laugh again. I learned that nothing is so serious that life should stop because of it. I learned that even with the bad there's always good. I learned to laugh at life's absurdities and to laugh at myself. I started to do things with my life. I started to write. I started an after-school group for my daughter and some other girls, recruited some teenage volunteers, and now I get to hang out with teenage girls once a week. (I don't mind the hair and the nails, but the music drives me crazy.) I learned that life can be fun, even when it's not what you planned on.

I learned to laugh again. I learned that nothing is so serious that life should stop because of it.

In spite of her disability, Kate has always been very healthy. Then last year we had a new experience. Our troops got to go on maneuvers. Kate got to experience surgery to straighten her spine and I got to experience hell on earth. She had a 117-degree curve in a spine that's supposed to be straight. Using my rediscovered sense of humor, I started calling her "pretzel girl." But it really wasn't funny. It was terrifying.

I started having anxiety attacks—heart palpitations, chest pains, crying jags. I was put on antidepressants, which allowed me to be terrified without breaking down. Those lovely little pills got me through the next six months of her surgery and then her recovery. Thanks to my other antidepressant, chocolate, I also gained forty pounds. A nice reminder of the event, which I still carry around with me.

Kate did make it through this very dangerous surgery, fully recovered without incident, and now has a straight spine. She was even able to sit on the seat beside me in the van going home, which was a dream come true for my wheelchair-bound daughter.

Kate and I spent six months recovering from surgery together. The first two months she was at home with me and wasn't happy about it. As I dutifully doled out painkillers that didn't do much, and tried to find ways to keep her mind off her discomfort, she felt it her duty to share with me how she felt about the situation. She hurt. She was bored. She couldn't lie comfortably on her stomach anymore. Her incisions were itching. She wanted to be entertained. She wanted to go to the mall. She wanted to be anywhere else but here. So did I. She cried. I cried. Then we looked at each other and both burst out laughing at how ridiculous we were being. So we cheered up by going to the mall and eating chocolate together. Best painkiller around, combined with a wonderful mother-daughter bonding experience.

I don't compare Kate to non-disabled girls her age anymore. I'm content to be the mom of this wonderful young woman. Her disability is part of who she is. Sometimes I do get a hint of that bittersweet feeling of what life might have been, but somehow it doesn't seem so important anymore. Kate has had and will have her milestones to celebrate. Although I wouldn't have believed it years ago, those celebrations are as sweet as any others could be. Kate has had her first date (her worker went along), her first kiss (her worker held her up), and her first dance (yes, with her worker in tow). We've also celebrated the first anniversary of her spinal surgery and the first time she took a step as we held her up. She was twelve and we cheered until we were hoarse. Do I feel sad that we have to celebrate such things? Surprisingly, no. These truly are celebrations for us.

So now I'm career army. No promotions. No decorations. No medals. Lots of hard work. What do I get out of it? I get to eat chocolate at the mall. And I get to drive the van with Kate sitting beside me.

Dealing with the Tragedy of HB Syndrome

RICK HODGES

As THE FATHER of a child with the common genetic disorder known as Down syndrome, I have learned about all kinds of disabilities affecting children. I was shocked to learn, though, that the most common genetic problem striking millions of children today gets very little attention—Human Being syndrome (HBS).

HBS is a genetic condition that is passed on from parents who carry the genes that cause it, though doctors still don't fully understand this process. Millions of people are carriers of the gene that causes the condition, though few carriers know they have it. Like many genetic conditions, children born with HBS can have a range of physical and mental problems. Tragically, millions of cases of HBS go undiagnosed.

If you have ever wondered why your son or daughter is acting strange, or ever said "What's wrong with you?" to your child, you may have a case of HBS on your hands.

Symptoms that parents of HBS children can expect throughout their child's development include the following: hyperactivity, short attention span, disputes and fights with siblings and friends, poor hearing when spoken to by a parent, lapses in memory (especially when required to do chores or homework), sluggishness in the teenage years, and general irresponsibility.

Most HBS victims suffer from minor diseases, such as colds and flu, and a few get serious and even fatal diseases. They will almost certainly require repeated visits to the doctor throughout their lives. HBS children are very susceptible to accidents causing injury, such as falling off bikes or getting hit by softballs. They may even have severe accidents, often involving skateboards, trampolines, or cars, causing permanent disability or death. They are particularly prone to problems in the teenage years, but their tendency toward poor judgment and lack of coordination is apparent from a very early age.

HBS children are also at risk of becoming addicted to drugs. The medical reasons for this are unclear, but the chemicals in some drugs seem to affect the brains of HBS sufferers, rendering them dependent on the substances. HBS children may also grow up to be criminals. A few cases have been reported of HBS children committing horrible violent crimes, but luckily these incidents are very rare.

Nevertheless, most children with HBS experience great anxiety adjusting to school life and fitting in with peer groups because of their condition. Mental and social problems can follow HBS children throughout their adult lives. Problems facing adult HBS sufferers include divorce, child abuse, alcoholism, mental illness, poverty, and suicide. If they survive these, all HBS sufferers degenerate mentally and physically as their age advances.

Fortunately there are treatments for HBS. Most communities have schools where children with HBS can receive intensive education and learn social skills in the process. Medical science has made amazing advances in the treatment of HBS-related problems in the past few decades. Thanks to modern medicine, broken bones and other injuries suffered by accident-prone children with HBS are now easily treated, and many diseases are handled with surgery or medication. Orthodontists have even developed special appliances that help straighten teeth, as they often grow crooked in children with HBS.

If your child has Human Being syndrome, don't despair. There are many other parents with children who have the same condition, and they can help. Seek their advice or join a support group. With hard work, patience, and help from family and friends, your child can grow up to lead a reasonably happy, normal life.

I believe the parents of children with disabilities should extend our hands to help parents of children stricken with HBS. And when you see them on the street, try not to stare. Just treat them like everyone else.

What's Your Name?

BERNADETTE THOMAS

AS HE STRETCHES OUT HIS HAND, he says, "Hi, my name's Richard. What's yours?"

This perfect stranger looked at my son, reluctantly offered her hand, and hesitantly said, "My name is Helen," hoping that would be the end of it. But alas—

"Hi, Helen. . . . Are you married? Do you have kids? Where do you live?"

Poor Helen didn't know what hit her. What was she to do? There was this little boy with Down syndrome looking at her, anxiously waiting to know the answers to his questions. She looked at me expectantly, that look that I have seen hundreds of times before, that look from strangers that says "Please rescue me."

I would look embarrassed and berate Richard for being so forward, trying to explain to him that it was not polite to ask people, particularly strangers, such personal questions. He would look at me all confused and say, "But you do, Mom." What could I say, my son not only has the Down's gene, he also has my genes. He is inquisitive like me, he likes people like I do, and he also has a bit of pizzazz—modestly, I have to say, just like I do.

So why did I get embarrassed? Well, probably because I was embarrassed about having a child with Down syndrome, a child who really didn't fit into the world. A child who looks a little funny, a child who can speak really well, a child who is demanding, a child who is intellectually challenged. This child who asks strangers personal questions is my child.

Eventually, though, it occurred to me that the many "Helens" we had met over the last eleven years were actually okay about answering questions. I started to relax and stopped rescuing people from the barrage of Richard questions. And you know what? I even started to laugh at how silly it all was. So what if a disabled kid asked you if you are married? Big deal! I no longer felt the panic or the shame. I started to see life in a brighter light. It was like the mist started to rise and I could see the sun again. It felt good to laugh.

I started to laugh not just at myself but also at my son, and the best part was that I didn't feel guilty about it. Very early on I tried to be an advocate for political correctness when it came to all things "disabled." And that was a good thing and certainly served a purpose, but I lost sight of who I was. The "me" before Richard came along had laughed at everything; nothing was sacred. The "me" after Richard came along was so serious that it smothered the laughter within and caused me all sorts of emotional problems. I lost track of a fundamental part of my personality because I didn't think I had the right to laugh at anything anymore. But the funny thing was that Richard was not serious at all. If he could laugh, why couldn't I?

I would allow myself to laugh in the privacy of my own safety. I would sometimes look at Richard with his little tongue hanging out, drooling a little from the side of his mouth, his eyes looking blissfully at each other and that vacant "off with the pixies" look, and I would have to laugh—"Hello, is anyone there?" I know that may sound a little harsh, and I still don't know if it was nervous laughter, but it made me laugh. It made me laugh to think that, at that moment, he was totally oblivious to anything in the world, and it also made me feel better. For all the worrying I did about my son's future, what people thought of him and me, he really didn't care about any of those things. He seemed perfectly content and happy.

I would allow myself to laugh when I would catch a glimpse of myself, sour-faced with rage when someone said something politically incorrect. In the past it was me who usually put my foot in it, and I would laugh then, so why can't I laugh now? I felt good about laughing at myself and laughing at the serious me, and it felt good to laugh at what my life had turned into. No way in the world would I have wanted this life. It's tough at times, but here I am and here I will stay, and I may as well enjoy the ride.

I can now laugh at the silly things Richard does. I laugh when he puts his T-shirt on back to front for the umpteenth time, no matter how many times I say "tag at the back." He still doesn't get it. I can now laugh when he still puts his right shoe on his left foot and vice versa. I don't start crying because he can't, I start laughing because he doesn't care—it still fits! I can now laugh that he starts to sing out loud in a crowded movie theater. I don't shrivel up and tell him to be quiet—now I join in. I can now laugh that he says the most inappropriate things at the most inappropriate times. I can laugh and the Politically Correct police won't come down and take me to prison. And, most importantly, I don't feel embarrassed.

I can laugh and the Politically Correct police won't come and take me to prison.

I used to put such huge expectations on myself as a mother, particularly as the mother of a disabled child. I don't do that anymore. I have given myself a pat on the back, knowing I am not perfect, nor is my son—but then, who is? I'm not saying it is always easy, but at the end of the day I have a wonderful, warm, funny, caring child who is a little slow at times, and at the end of the day Richard has a mother who is wonderful, warm, funny, caring, and a little slow at times. We love each other and we fit into this world in our own happy way.

ACKNOWLEDGMENTS

This book has been on my mind for so many years, and at the end of the day I doubt very much if I ever would have completed it without Cindy coming on board. I am eternally grateful for her professionalism, her wisdom, and most of all her humor. It has been a wonderful journey.

A big thank you to Neil for adding the voice of reason to these pages.

To all the people we e-mailed and spoke to all around the world in order to get these stories, we thank you and your associations. Without you this book would have not been possible. There are far too many of you to mention individually, but you know who you are. Thank you so much for supporting us with enthusiasm and good grace. We have made some wonderful friends through this journey, and it is reassuring to know that the disability community is full of so many caring and loving individuals.

To our friends and families who spread the word, thank you.

To Anna Stewart, Deborah Tobias, Sara Haddad, Erica Hatcher, Jill O'Connor—thanks for your help.

A heartfelt thanks to Keller Johnson and the Helen Keller Foundation, the copyright holders, for the use of Helen's poem, "Let Us Have Faith." If you would like to know more about the great work they do, look up www.helenkellerfoundation.org.

To my husband, Gareth, thank you so much—your love and support have meant everything.

We also thank most deeply our publishers and their staff. It is a compassionate company that can see the benefit of a book such as ours as a useful book to help people in our communities.

To all the parents that wrote to us—this book would not have been possible without you, and you are indeed very brave women and men opening up your lives to be viewed by so many. It is the hardest task in the world to write about your own life and feelings, but you have done it and done it so well. And to their children— no matter what your parents have written, they love you with all their hearts. They respect your right to live a full and dignified life, and will fight till the end to achieve that.

And, most importantly, the biggest thank-you must go to Cindy's and my boys, Nicholas and Richard. You make us laugh, you make us cry, but most of all you make us love so deeply. You are our inspiration.

—BERNADETTE THOMAS

Appendix

How Some Parents Unwind

My son, Erik, has helped me to realize the truth that is ours to tell. A truth that says we are all created equal, despite, race, disability, or creed. Once a person has found their reason for being here, there is no turning back. Advocacy is the truth that I must tell. To that end, we have established Advocates Needed Today Inc. (www.AdvocatesNeededToday.org), a nonprofit corporation that educates, supports, and mentors families and people with disabilities to live meaningful lives in the community of their choice, with the support services needed to do so. We have found our truth to tell, and tell it we do, with exuberance.

— Rebecca Riggs

As much as I adore our Down syndrome teenage son, I also need "me-time." I am fortunate to have a talent for digital art and poetry. It is wonderful to sit at my computer and connect with something deep inside my soul as the artwork flows onto the screen. Similarly, a poem will bubble out of my head, and I receive great satisfaction when it expresses a hitherto nebulous thought pattern. The buzz I get from selling a picture or having a poem published is tremendous.

— Rose-Mary Gower

I choose not to let myself be defined by my children's disabilities, for it's not what they become that will determine my success in life, but what I become. Through my experiences, I've become a teacher to others. With compassion and respect, I teach the schools that educate my children, for I realize how difficult it is to recognize and understand the impact of a social disability on an intellectually superior child. To teach parents of children with Asperger's syndrome, I run a Yahoo Internet support list, http://health.groups.yahoo.com/group/aspergerparentsupport. Additionally, I wrote a poem, "The Misunderstood Child," that has opened many hearts. Open hearts mean open minds. My children have opened my heart. And I embrace my life with them.

— KATHY WINTERS

Parenting a child with a chronic, progressive illness requires astounding courage. In order to formulate the right balance of grit and compassion, I envision life through my son's eyes. What kind of a parent would I want to help me bear my situation? One who felt sorry for me? Sometimes. One who'd let me feel sorry for myself? Not really. Would my parent persevere with me through the highs and lows this disease brings? Always. Walking in my son's shoes does not provide all the insight I need to forge ahead. Good friends listen to my highs and lows. An Internet cystic fibrosis group offers information about issues including insurance, school, and emotional support. Many members have CF, and they are a great resource and inspiration.

— KATHERINE KRISHNAN

I think the things that sustain our family and help us to thrive are the small and seemingly ordinary parts of an ordinary day. We try to focus on how ordinary we are rather than always having to be in the category of "special." This is boosted by maintaining a healthy sense of humor and realizing that everything my two "special" children do is *not* so special; they are like their typically developing peers in many ways. Rather than crying over spilled juice, I patiently wipe it up. Rather then yelling about the sticky hands in my hair and the jam all over their faces, I look at my oldest child—now almost eighteen, almost grown—and remember the days she did the same. I remember that broken crayons can be replaced, but broken spirits may never mend. So rather than always staying in the special-ness of my special-needs children, I have chosen to see how wonderful we *each* are and how much each of my children has taught me. They have taught me to love without condition and pray without ceasing, and most of all, to appreciate each moment and realize we are each simply being ourselves.

— Zan Liccone

I think the best thing I do to unwind and renew my spirit is pray and meditate on all the good things in my life. I remember to thank God for all he has given me. I pray for wisdom and tolerance often. I also have a very strong support system of friends who have kids with autism. We go out frequently. We try to find humor in our lives and to share it with one another. I love to go to concerts. Music in my house is of the classic rock-and-roll type, and is played loud and often. You might even find me dancing while I'm cleaning my house. I have also been known to write a poem every now and then. I guess in my heart I always wanted to be a songwriter, and I have really never given up that dream. My husband and I have a great time joking around with each other. The reason I have a good attitude about life is due to prayer and humor. Without these I'm not sure how I would survive.

— Tina Rivenbark

I love dipping into something that's totally unrelated to my life. I religiously stay away from self-help books and inspiring true-life stories—they depress me no end (maybe some of it's too close to home). Instead, I love losing myself in a great book—mysteries and whodunnits are my favorite, but fantasy and fiction are a close second. In the evenings I unwind with a good drama on television—action thrillers and, yes, soppy love stories also make good watching for me. But I make it a rule to only watch happily-ever-after movies—that's why I haven't seen *Titanic* yet!

But over and above all of these, my pet pastime is doing crossword puzzles, which are great last thing at night. I always have several on the go. It's what I dip into when I get a few minutes for a cup of tea or some time to myself. My favorite time is after the kids are in bed and I finally have the evening to myself. Then, no matter how tired I am, I always stay up as late as I can to make the evening last that much longer . . . so that I can do my favorite things.

— SHARON PERERA

I started reading and writing, and finally gained courage to stand up and speak. I shared our experience to help "special" moms and dads so that they might be able to avoid the pain we went through. My son's various accomplishments became an inspiration and resource for us. He was the reason for my published papers, speeches, and workshops (see www.sujeet.com). Our mission now is to send the following message: "Hiding is not the answer. Take time to recognize your special children's hidden talents, help them to explore so that they can improvise with their disability to live a better life." It's never an easy path for parents, but the reward is that the joy your children bring becomes the re-fueling you need in life.

— DR. SINDOOR DESAI

The best way for me to be lifted out of a rut is to talk with another parent who has a child with Down syndrome. These treasured moments may come in many forms, and often I do not consciously seek them out, but rather they are sent to me. It may be that I meet a complete stranger, or visit with a friend who has a child with Down syndrome; and at times my best and most treasured contacts have come as a combination of both. This is what I call "the Internet stranger/friend," a true support person who gets me through the challenges, but who may be in another country and whom I may never meet. No matter where the support comes from, it always seems to come at just the right time from just the right place. I like the following websites: www.nads.org and www.unomas21.com.

— LISA DEPPERMAN

When the blood leaves the pit of my stomach, leaving a void of fear and futility, I paint. I don't think, I just paint. It moves the empty spot to my head from which it is eventually able to escape— like a liberated balloon.

—DON WARD

I have vowed to make a difference for parents who follow in my path. I was recently given an advisory-committee position for our state's special-needs insurance. I have also volunteered with hospital social workers to be a parent support contact should they feel it would help new parents to speak with someone.

I have found much solace in creative activities and have recently started a home-based business that is helping me to apply my talents as well as to learn new skills. My husband and I are organizing an annual golf outing to raise money and awareness for a craniofacial organization. It's gratifying to raise the money, but it's even more important to have so many friends and family gather in support of one's own family.

My psychotherapist has been instrumental in my recovery program. Once you admit that you can't go it alone anymore, be sure to reach out to family and friends. And obtaining the outside opinion of a therapist of some kind (social worker, religious counselor, and so on), if possible, to weigh in on one's sanity is very nice. A private journal can also become an excellent outlet and good friend during your darkest hours. It allows you to express your feelings in a safe environment. I have found that my journal, which I leave and come back to sometimes several months between visits, is a very good way to check in with myself and document feelings that I may forget about years from now. Feeling better mentally and emotionally has enabled me to take steps toward improving my physical self. After my first try at a yoga class, I realized how much the physical, mental, and emotional elements are all connected.

Working through the process of grief and coming to a point of acceptance is only the beginning. At that point you are finally able to look up and take a step forward. Where you take that step or steps, though, is entirely your choice. Be sure to take them wisely, with great thought, and with extreme compassion for yourself.

—DEDE DANKELSON

I am the editor of the newsletter for a parent-to-parent organization for families raising children with special needs. I have proudly grown into my role as the mother of a child with special needs and become not only an advocate but a champion for all those who color outside the lines. Our group shares a deep intimacy even though some of us barely know each other. When we sit around a table, celebrating our successes, supporting our struggles, and solving our issues, I know that I am in the company of my clan, bound beyond time and space.

How do I refuel? Though I take good care of myself, I am never as free of my worries as when I dance. Occasionally I can find the release in my living room, dancing to Santana, but more likely it is in a dance studio, the music loud, and me and my fellow dancers undulating to rhythms inside and out. In the dance I am reminded of my divinity, and take delight in the lightness of my being as I dance on the edge between heaven and earth.

—ANNA STEWART

I guess the best way I find to make the most of my life is to spend time with my great circle of friends. They can give life perspective and clarity when things seem to be going wrong. Some of these friends have a child with a disability. Most do not, but in my experiences I have learned that we all have issues with our kids in some way or another. I also work in a field where I have a lot of social contact with lots of people from different age groups and walks of life. It is true that there is always someone worse off than yourself, and I have found that realization to be invaluable in times of desperation.

The group of parents at the school that my son attends is a great source of inspiration, and we all assist each other with different treatments and therapies that have been tried by the various families. I don't think you can beat having a positive attitude concerning your family's situation and knowing that you are doing the best you possibly can for your child.

— CAROLYN FENNELL

Battery-charging comes in different forms for everyone. For me what works best is daily yoga meditation practiced in the early morning when everyone else is still sleeping. For that short time I can cultivate the fantasy that I live in an exquisitely peaceful retreat, perhaps on some utterly gorgeous—and remote—Hawaiian island. And there I practice my meditation. That time alone is my touchstone with my own reality, my own truth.

When I'm there, I know that everything really will be all right in the end; that this whole divine "movie" that I'm living out in daily life was perhaps arranged so that I could learn how-tos. Such as how to keep my peace no matter what, how to take care of myself and get some R&R. Whatever works, we owe it to that truth-knowing Self to do it. A cup of tea, a book, and a blanket; a bag of popcorn and a good film; a long walk in the park; or whatever it takes for us to recapture our vision of the big picture and our warm, everything-will-be-all-right place in it. Because everything really will be all right.

— NATALIE HALE

The longest amount of time I spend away from my children is at work. I am an RN. It is a nice break to be around people who work well together as a team and are supportive and *organized*! My goodness, all three things together at one time and consistent. A rarity in my house!

I do enjoy books when I can read them, but mostly I listen to tapes while I drive. I do like to go to the movies alone and with my children. It is just as rewarding to be alone and quiet, too. These are my favorite websites: http://Schwablearning.org and www.wrightslaw.com. I like to read and respond to posts on these sites.

— SANDY MILLER

During the initial raw months, the first movie (at my mother's urging) was the newly released *Forrest Gump*. It was possibly the best movie to watch at the time as it made us laugh and cry and even gave us hope in its own quirky way. I liked my husband's interpretation of the movie. He said the movie portrayed all the main characters, not just Forrest Gump, as having some kind of disability. With Forrest Gump it was his intellect, his childhood sweetheart had a psychological disability, and his best friend had a physical disability. In life, who is to say what is "normal" and what is not!

— Shona Parekh

I can't adequately take care of my family's needs (plus Cassidy's special needs) if I don't take care of myself. I've learned not to feel guilty about taking some time to be by myself and regroup. I love to do scrapbooking (to feel like I'm getting something done!) and I enjoy reading (it's nice to escape to another world from time to time!). But surprisingly, one of the most helpful things I've found is communicating on the Internet with other parents of children with special needs. The encouragement, support, experience, and vast amounts of information I've received from other parents has been a priceless gift that I never dreamed would be such a help! Parent support groups for almost any and every disability out there can be found at www.our-kids.org and Yahoo Groups.

— Cheryl Veenstra

Simply getting out of the house for brief periods of time can be helpful. Leaving the stressful surroundings, if only to visit a bookstore to take in a cup of tea and enjoy the serenity of a soothing and relaxing environment, or take a walk around the block, often makes the return to caretaking more tolerable. Finding individuals who can provide regular and trusted in-home child care assistance is essential. Even if you can't leave your home, you could turn your bathroom into an inexpensive mini-spa while the sitter takes over caring for your child.

Activities such as exercise, reading, and crafts are also good stress relievers, as is massage therapy. An excellent online support group link is www.kidpower.com. This online group is well established and offers educational resources while providing a venue for parents to share experiences, frustrations, and triumphs with other parents of children with disabilities.

Another helpful outlet is community respite providers. After an interview with the respite providers where the special circumstances of the child are discussed, parents leave their special-needs child and siblings, free of charge, and go off to spend the evening however they choose.

— MICHELLE MARKLE

How do I cope with parenting a disabled daughter? I laugh a lot. Humor is my sanity. It allows me to accept the absurdities of this life I live with my sweet Kate without collapsing under the very heavy load I carry at times. I have to laugh at the absurdities of this life. Of knowing more than I ever wanted to about neurology, nonverbal communication, advocacy, wheelchair repair, accessibility, begging for funding, drool control, nutrition, adult diapers— the list goes on. When I take a step back and look at it all, it's pretty ridiculous. And laughing sure beats crying. I cried for years. Enough is enough.

I've learned how to see through the surface to what's inside people, and that gift enriches my life incredibly. "Civilians" miss so much. The usual things—money, status, appearance—just don't matter. Oh, and I gave up control. I don't try to control what I can't and I don't worry about the future. I plan, yes. But I live for today. I accept what is, and know it's as it should be. Strong faith and strong love. That's how I cope. My life is good.

— ELLEN FORREST

Authors' Notes

Page xi ". . . 7.5 million members of the U.S. population can be classified as 'retarded'": U.S. population census 1990, quoted in "Introduction to Mental Retardation," The Arc of the United States, 2002. See www.thearc.org/info-mr.html.

Page xii ". . . one in every 100 children will be born with an autism spectrum disorder": L. Wing, "Autistic Spectrum Disorders," *British Medical Journal* 312 (1996): 327–28.

Page xii "A thousand individuals are born with cystic fibrosis . . .": Cystic Fibrosis Foundation, "What is CF?," May 2003. See www.cff.org/about_cf/what_is_cf/.

Page xii ". . . ten children in every ten thousand live births will have Down syndrome": Center for Disease Control and Prevention, *Morbidity and Mortality Weekly Report* 43, no. 33 (August 26, 1994): 617–22. See www.cdc.gov/mmwr/preview/mmwrhtml/00032401.htm.

Page xii "In the United Kingdom, . . .": The U.K. statistics are from the following sources: *Hearing impairment:* The Royal National Institute for Deaf People (RNID) website, www.rnid.org.uk 2002, "Facts and Figures on Deafness and Tinnitus"; *Blindness:* Royal National Institute for the Blind (RNIB), www.rnib.org.uk, "Statistics on Sight Problems in the UK"; *Cerebral Palsy and the total number of disabled:* SCOPE website, www.scope.org.uk, "An Introduction to Disability Issues," August 2001.

Page xii ". . . and 1,800 babies are diagnosed with cerebral palsy every year": March of Dimes, Professionals and Researchers Quick Reference and Fact Sheets. Last updated July 21, 2003. See www.marchofdimes.com/professionals/681_1208.asp.

Page xii ". . . three in a thousand will be born with a significant hearing impairment": National Center on Birth Defects and Developmental

Disabilities, the Early Hearing and Intervention (EHDI) program. December 17, 2002. See www.cdc.gov/ncbddd/dd/ddhi.htm.

Page 5 "First suggested by Olshansky . . ." S. Olshansky, "Chronic Sorrow: A Response to Having a Mentally Defective Child," *Social Change Magazine* 43 (1962): 191–94.

Page 76 "Research from the U.S.-based Depression and Related Affective Disorders Association (DRADA) reveal . . .": Depression and Related Affective Disorders Association, 2002. See www.hopkinsmedicine.org.

Page 195 "A recent study published in *The Medical Journal of Australia* found strong links between an individual's religious conviction and their longevity": Kelly Burke, "In God We Trust to Live Happier and Healthier," *Sydney Morning Herald,* January 21, 2003.

Page 195 "Similarly, the Center for the Study of Religion/Spirituality and Health at Duke University has conducted several studies . . .": H. Helm, J. C. Hays, E. Flint, H. G. Koenig, D. G. Blazer (2000). "Effects of Private Religious Activity on Mortality of Elderly Disabled and Non-disabled Adults," *Journal of Gerontology* (Medical Sciences) 55A, M400–M405.

Page 222 "Laughter reduces stress. Researchers at Loma Linda University in California found that immune function . . .": Drs. Lee Berk and Stan Tan, first published September–October 1996 issue of *Humor and Health Journal,* published by the Humor and Health Institute, Van Nuys, California.

BIBLIOGRAPHY

Boss, Pauline. *Ambiguous Loss: Learning to Live with Unresolved Grief.* Cambridge, Mass.: Harvard University Press, 1999.

Cox, Gary, Robert Bendiksen, and Robert Stevenson. *Complicated Grieving and Bereavement: Understanding and Treating People Experiencing Loss.* New York: Baywood Publishing, 2002.

McKissock, Mal, and Dianne McKissock. *Coping with Grief.* Sydney, Aus.: ABC Books, 1985.

Rogers, Carl. *Client-Centred Therapy: Its Current Practice, Implications, and Theory.* London: Constable and Robinson, 1976.

Sprang, Ginny, and John McNeil. *The Many Faces of Bereavement: The Nature and Treatment of Natural, Traumatic and Stigmatized Grief.* New York: Bruner/Mazel, 1999.

Westberg, Granger. *Good Grief.* Minneapolis: Augsburg Fortress Press, 1979.

Recommended Reading

Bluebond-Langer, Myra. *In the Shadow of Illness: Parents and Siblings of the Chronically Ill Child*. Princeton, N.J.: Princeton University Press, 1996.

Gill, Barbara. *Changed by a Child: Companion Notes for Parents of a Child with a Disability*. New York: Broadway, 1997.

Klein, Stanley, and Kim Schive, eds. *You Will Dream New Dreams: Inspiring Personal Stories by Parents of Children with Disabilities*. New York: Kensington, 2001.

Miller, Nancy B. *Nobody's Perfect: Living and Growing with Children Who Have Special Needs*. Baltimore: Brookes Publishing, 1994.

Naseef, Robert A. *Special Children, Challenged Parents: The Struggles and Rewards of Raising a Child with a Disability*. Baltimore: Brookes Publishing, 2001.

Senator, Susan. *Making Peace with Autism: One Family's Story of Struggle, Discovery, and Unexpected Gifts*. Boston: Shambhala, 2005.

Strohm, Kate. *Being the Other One: Growing Up with a Brother or Sister Who Has Special Needs*. Boston: Shambhala, 2005.

RESOURCES

The Arc of the United States (www.thearc.org)

A national organization of and for people with mental retardation and related developmental disabilities and their families, devoted to promoting and improving support and services.

Brave Kids (www.bravekids.org)

Resources for children with chronic, life-threatening diseases or disabilities including information on therapies, camps, legal advice, home health care, support groups, and more.

Exceptional Parent (www.exceptionalparent.com)

A magazine and website that provide information, support, ideas, encouragement, and outreach for parents and families of children with disabilities, and the professionals who work with them.

Woodbine House (www.woodbinehouse.com)

Offers a wide variety of books on special needs for parents, children, and professionals.

INDEX